Living Fulfilled

The Infectious Joy of Serving Others

Eleze "Lisa" Thomas–McMillan

foodbankcarlisa@yahoo.com

Living Fulfilled . . . The Infectious Joy of Serving Others
Copyright 2015 by Eleze "Lisa" Thomas-McMillan

ISBN: 1-885091-08-7
Library of Congress Control Number: 2014916920
Book cover design by Matias DC
Matias.delcarmine@gmail.com
Book design by: Julie Kalinowski
juliekalinowski@yahoo.com
Edited by: Mark Weising

Printed in United States of America
First Edition 2015
www.pleasebelievepeoplearehungry.com

To my parents, Earlie Ray Thomas (1907–2007) and Bertha Lee Thomas (1921–2010); to my son, General Lee Marshall Thomas; and to my wonderful husband, Freddie, without whose encouragement and support my work would not be possible and this book would not have been possible.

Table of Contents

Introduction

For the past seventeen years, I have had the privilege of living my dream. With God's assistance, I have helped loosen the chains of poverty, hunger, hopelessness, and despair for people in need of a little kindness. I am so grateful to God for allowing me a small part in His mission.

I walked 110 miles in 2004 and 900 miles in 2005 in an effort to spread awareness for the scores of hungry, often unrecognized, people who surround us. My message to those I met on my journey was simple: *no one should ever have to go hungry.* I invite you to share my broader dream of a world in which everyone strives to live for others. My philosophy is this: if we all live for one another instead of for ourselves, no one will go hungry or have to endure the many sufferings that accompany a life of poverty.

If that sounds naïve, all I can say is this is the only approach to suffering that makes sense to me. In these pages, I will outline some of the events on my journey that informed this vision and describe the simple ways in which we can respond to the needs of those around us. Often, help needn't be a large donation or grand gesture. A few dollars, an offer to lend a hand, or even just a small smile can go a long way toward healing some of the world's ills. My hope is to demonstrate that this is a truly rewarding and joyous way to live and to inspire you to also dedicate your time and resources to those who desperately need your help.

To begin, pick a place that is right for you. At the end of this memoir, I have provided a list of suggestions to help you figure out how to start your own journey. Give where you can, when you can. Know that the blessings you bestow on others will heal the walking wounded and help your own rivers flow with abundance and joy.

A willing poor man can do just as much with his resources as a reluctant rich one. There are all kinds of ways to help. I hope some of the means described on the following pages will inspire you to be thankful for your blessings and pay them forward.

—Eleze "Lisa" Thomas-McMillan

PART I

Finding My Way

CHAPTER ONE

Roots and Wings

As a young black child growing up in Brewton, Alabama, I learned that although God provided, it was often a struggle to get one's hands on His rich provisions. Sharing the little we had was part of our everyday existence. It was as natural to us as inhaling the dust of the untarred roads.

Fourteen of us squeezed into a six-room wooden house that my dad and granddad built. My dad worked three jobs to support his family—digging ditches for the city, raising pigs and selling them at market, and hauling cotton pickers to the cotton fields in Florida.

We fed the pigs expired food discarded by a local grocery store, and all us children took turns helping out. I learned years later that much of the food the store manager let Dad take was still good to eat, so he brought some home and donated the rest to other families in the neighborhood. Claudie Gulley, a childhood friend, told me—her face glowing with delight—that her family hadn't known what cheese was until my dad gave them some. Dad was also an avid hunter. When he went into the woods on those cold winter nights, I think he always had in mind that it was more than his family he was trying to feed.

Apart from that, my folks did not even have enough of the basics to donate to the needy—my first bed was an old trunk—but the one thing they did have in abundance was children. My mom took great pleasure in loaning us out to other people in the community, especially older people. We would clean for them, spend the night if they were alone, and cook for them, or just visit when they needed company. Mom gave us strict instructions not to charge them, but we were able to make a little extra money in other ways. In the fall we picked and sold scuppernongs, and we did other little odd jobs around town like shelling peas for people who could afford to pay a small token of fifty cents or a dollar, which was big money to us.

When Dad hauled cotton pickers to the cotton fields, we were the cotton pickers! Every summer from the age of six, we all knew what we were going to be doing, and we were never happy about it. All we had to look forward to was getting up at four in the morning, freezing on the back of Dad's old truck, and suffering through a sweltering day in the fields. In the morning the dew was so heavy on the plants that my pant legs would get soaking wet and muddy. It just felt yucky! We longed for a summer when we could be like other kids and just enjoy our summer break.

In the fields, we had long sacks hanging on our shoulders that we dragged behind us and stuffed with cotton. Our hands throbbed from the pricks of the cotton pods. When the sack seemed full or became too heavy to drag, we would take it to the weigh station. The actual weight was usually a huge letdown, because the sacks always felt a lot heavier than the scales said they were. We suspected they had rigged their equipment.

It was not all bad. I forgot all the hardship when boys like Milton and our next-door neighbor Bubba came with us. They were funny, kind country boys with hearts of gold and ever so nice to talk to. Oh, those first crushes are always the sweetest! We also enjoyed visiting the local neighborhood store at lunchtime to buy our favorite snacks—cinnamon rolls, bologna, and Coca-Cola—which we ate and drank sitting under a big pine tree, talking and enjoying each other's company. On the way home in the evening, we would lie on the bed of the truck as we approached our home to avoid being seen by the other kids, knowing they would tease us if they saw us. At the end of the workday on Saturday, we would line up to get paid.

With the little money I made, I managed to buy a few school clothes and shoes. Still, despite these perks, my siblings and I celebrated with much delight when they invented cotton-picking machinery. You would have thought we were going to get royalties on each bale they harvested! We were happy we could start school on the first day like the other kids and not be in the cotton fields, and we were glad there would be no more hiding on the back of Dad's truck.

Much to our father's annoyance, all his hard work was not always enough to meet our needs, so Mom began taking odd jobs to help out. I didn't understand his attitude at the time, but I reckon he was from a generation where men were the providers and women stayed home to look after the kids and take care of the household. A working wife would maybe give the impression that as a father and husband he was not doing his duty. Ooh, you should have heard him cuss!

When I was seven years old, Mom got a job hoeing butterbeans for a week. She and I were dressed and ready to go by dawn, and when she got into the truck, I crawled over her lap to sit between her and Dad. I knew she was not going to make me get out because she liked the company. Mom did the hard work with the hoe, always checking carefully that there were no snakes around. I would follow close behind, making sure all the weeds were up. By the time my father picked us up at dusk, Mom's hands were blistered and calloused. When we got home, she soaked them and nodded off as I gently rubbed them in the warm water.

I treasured that time in the bean field, especially being close to Mom when we sat down to eat the fried egg sandwiches she had brought from home. It was the only time I had my mom to myself. She made five dollars a day for that job and used it to buy socks and school supplies. Those days with Mom were great, but there were also days that proved to be not so fun, because there was little play time and lots of hard work time.

There were plenty of times my dad spanked me, too, but the memory I treasure the most is the one time he tried to save me and my sisters from a whipping. That day my mom took my younger sisters, Molly and Annette, and me to get our shots. Dad dropped us off about eight o'clock, and as we slowly climbed the many steps to the health department, we girls took the smallest steps we could to slow down the process. My mother gave us the speech about not acting crazy. She was a no-nonsense person when it came to situations she felt would embarrass her. We girls we were terrified of shots. We hated needles!

Finally, to our regret, we reached the top of the stairs and Mom began to open the door. I do not know which one of us ran first, but we all decided that running was the right thing to do and took off in three different directions. When I looked behind me, I saw my sisters running and heard my mom yelling for us to come back. I knew we were in big trouble. Standing on the corner, I watched her chase down and tackle my younger sister Molly under a big bush on the courthouse lawn. I could see Molly's little buckteeth glistening as she screamed at the top of her voice for Mom not to whip her and to not make her take the shots. Mom was saying, "You get out from under this bush. Embarrassing me in front of all these people!" I thought, what people? I didn't see any people.

Finally, Mom started back across the courtyard with Molly—now looking like a limp rag doll—in tow. After parking Molly on the steps and ordering her not to move, Mom spotted Annette hiding behind a big green car in the parking lot. Mom approached the car and ordered Annette to stand up and come to her, because she knew Annette was the runner in the family. Every time a spanking was coming to us, Annette would take off running. Mom would get so angry at her that it would make it easier for the rest of us, because our whooping would not be so bad if Annette's was double for running.

On this day, Annette did not mind Mom. Instead, she went the opposite way around the car. Around and around they went, circling the vehicle until I got dizzy watching them. Finally, with one big thrust, Mom reached her arms as far as she could, grabbed Annette, tugged her to the steps, and ordered her not to move. Mom could not take a chance on leaving the "runner," so she held on to Annette, looked down the block, spotted me, and ordered me to come to her. I knew she meant business. She was so mad. She kept telling us how embarrassed she was and that our father was going to whoop us good.

Finally we went in and did the "no-shot shuffle" with the nurses—that's when you keep moving your arm back and forth to avoid the needle, but then, of course, they finally stick you and in a few seconds it is over, and you wonder what all the fuss was about. You cannot explain it, but you know the same thing will happen the next time. We all tried to enjoy that wonderful moment when the shot was over, but we knew nothing was going to stop Mom from telling Dad how we had behaved.

When Dad turned the corner at the courthouse to pick us up, Mom was still fuming. She was so mad and embarrassed that she was spitting bubbles as she told Dad what happened. We all listened and waited in mortal fear, but to everyone's surprise—including Mom's—Dad thought it was funny and laughed his head off. We laughed, too. If Dad was happy, we were happy. He told my mom to just leave us alone. Wow, I thought, *what a dad*. That moment changed my entire opinion of him.

His opinion, however, did not change my mom's mind. She was determined to spank us. After all, we had embarrassed her, and that was a big no-no. My dad never found out that as soon as he dropped us off at home and drove away, our mom gave us a whooping anyway. She began by telling each of us to go get a switch. Now, you had to use your head when it came to getting a switch. It was a serious task. Mom would not let you bring back just any ol' small, weak switch. It had to be up to the job.

When my mom started whooping us, our dog, Bullet, a gentle pit bull we had raised from a puppy, always tried to take the switch to stop her. Even though our little butts were getting beat, it was hard not to laugh when Bullet grabbed the hem of Mom's dress and pulled on it to get her to leave us alone. She looked really silly chasing her dress hem as she tried to get Bullet off. She would always have to take us in the house to finish the job. We loved Bullet, and we figured he saved our butts a little because Mom would get worn out trying to avoid him.

When I think about that day and how embarrassed my mom was, I always recall an episode that occurred years later. I had just returned home from my senior prom with my date, James. The prom was over at midnight, and we were in front of my house five minutes past midnight. As we sat there talking, I saw the shadow of a person coming around the car to the passenger side. I was startled, and when I looked out the window, I saw it was my mom. "Eleze, get out of that car and get in the house!" she yelled. I was horrified. I jumped out of the car, screaming and crying, and ran into the house. Now that was embarrassing. When I told my mom she had embarrassed me, she said life was full of embarrassing moments and that I would get over it. She was right. I did and moved on happily with my life.

My parents were strict, but they lived and toiled for us, and we were all expected to do our share. Their practical love left an impression deep inside of us that we were cherished, and that love meant sacrifice and hard labor. I knew without being told that I, the sixth kid in that gang of twelve, was worth the effort. Perhaps that is why I took it for granted that everyone else was worth the effort, too. As a result, it seemed quite normal that we kept only what we needed and gave the rest to others, even if all we had to give was our time and energy.

One of the most important and influential moments in my life happened when I was twelve years old. As I was walking home from my grandparents' house, coming up Fountain Avenue, a huge cloud of dust approached me. The closer I got to it, the clearer the image of a Cadillac became. I began to wave and smile at the white car, and it came to an abrupt stop right in front of me. A middle-aged white couple rolled the window down and called out to me, asking for my name.

"Eleze," I responded, "or Lisa for short."

The woman flashed her teeth at me in a huge smile. "That's a beautiful name. Thank you for being so polite and waving to us! Take this, dear, and always remember how important it is to be friendly. Don't ever change that." With that, she extended a closed fist and dropped something into my hand. It was a shiny Kennedy half-dollar!

"Th-thanks so much!" I said. I could hardly spit out the words. I immediately took off down the road, my heart racing, anxious to get home and tell my mom about this blessing.

When I showed Mom what the white couple had given me, she smiled and said, "You know, a lot of the neighbors have told me how nice you are—always smiling and waving at them when you pass." It struck me as odd that people made such a big deal out of someone just being friendly. I thought everybody waved. It still felt good to know that my friendliness was appreciated, though. The pure joy of that day stayed with me, and the fact that such a feeling was evoked through a simple act of friendliness left a lasting impression on me.

I also learned at a young age that caring for others involved pros and cons, pains and pleasures. From the age of about seven until I left home for college, my main source of freedom was serving as my grandparents' caregiver. I cooked and cleaned for them, and during the winter I made sure they had wood for the fire. No matter how cold it was, or how bad it was raining, or how I felt, they were my responsibility, and I took that responsibility seriously.

My grandfather (I called him Papa) was a sweet, gentle lamb. He would sit on the front porch in his big gray rocker and just watch the world go by. Every now and then he kept me entertained; our conversations were rare because he stuttered. On the other hand, Mama (my grandmother) was vociferous. She spoke her mind all the time, and even though I was the one who made sure they had what they needed, she treated me like a second-class citizen when their other children came to visit. The slight was noticeable, but I never said anything about it. No matter how badly it hurt my feelings, I did not want to take a chance on losing the freedom the visits gave me or risk losing the opportunity to visit my grandparents whenever I liked. I knew if I told my mom, she might have stopped me from going.

But, like most things, my freedom came with a price. To enjoy my time with my grandparents, I had to traverse "the block from hell" before and after school. I always called it that because somehow, regardless of which direction I went, I managed to find an angry dog that deemed my little butt perfect for a new chew toy.

However, by the time I was thirteen, I was more than happy to take a chance on the walk down that block. We had new neighbors—the Coin brothers, Bobby and June—and they were always waiting on the other side. The chance to flirt with them made everything worth it. Bobby Coin was the smoothest. I'll never forget the way my heart pounded in my neck the days I walked past their house and heard his raspy whistle, immediately followed by his gritty voice tickling my ears, saying, "I swear, you've got the prettiest legs." The compliment resonated with me the whole way home, only to be interrupted by the sound of my behind getting a nice beating from my dad for coming home late. That was usually what happened when I got involved with those Coin boys. They meant trouble for me, but I could not stay away.

One night, I was desperate to talk to Bobby. There was no phone in our house, so I figured I would just use my neighbor's. I slipped out of the house once my parents were fast asleep, around eleven, and made my way next door. Bobby and I talked and laughed for a few minutes, and I felt liberated. I do not even remember what time it was when I finally fell into my bed.

I woke up much earlier than I would have the next morning when my dad barged into my room. Apparently, our neighbor had decided to tell my parents about my late-night telephone call. I might have been able to save my butt from the vicious dogs in our neighborhood, but my dad was a completely different story! It sure was "bitten" that morning. But that didn't stop me from basking in the attention the Coin brothers showered on me. It was always a pleasant distraction from my dull life growing up in a small town in the South.

The excitement I felt just thinking of Bobby Coin made me want to live my young life to the fullest and share this newfound feeling. I wanted more—to share the joy of giving and receiving with anyone who was open to it—and I wanted to do more. I'd always treated people with kindness and had never hesitated to volunteer my time to help anyone I could, but I went at it with renewed vigor after getting the encouragement and gift from the white couple. It became a habit of mine to stop on the way home from school and offer assistance to my elderly neighbors.

Ms. Nellie, a frail woman in her eighties, became one of my regular stops. She looked after her five small grandchildren—those were some bad little demons! Every time I passed her house, I could hear them through the windows crying and fighting. So I was elated one day when she stopped me on my way home from school and asked for my help.

"Lisa!" I heard her soft, strained voice call from behind me.

"Hi, Ms. Nellie," I said. "How are you?"

She hesitated. "Do you think you could help me turn a mattress? Jessie stained it last night and I can't do it alone."

I entered her little worn wooden house through the side door. The house smelled of urine and was in terrible shambles. I could see the ground through the cracks in the floorboards. Even though we were all poor, I felt especially sad for Ms. Nellie.

She ushered her grandchildren outside to play while we took the urine-soaked linen off the mattress and turned it over. Once we had that done, I decided to sweep under the bed and clean up a little. I could see her trembling hands digging through her stained crusty apron pocket to find her little black coin purse.

After about fifteen minutes of cleaning and sweeping down spider webs, I said my goodbyes to her and her grandchildren. She thanked me and handed me four pennies. Some were so dirty you could not even see Lincoln's face on them. Four cents to a thirteen-year-old in the South during the 1960s was equivalent to a five-dollar bill today. As she put the pennies in my hand, I imagined all the things I could buy—a half bag of my favorite candy, four big sugar cookies, or, if I added one more penny, a nice soft yummy banana moon pie.

"Aw, that's real nice of you, Ms. Nellie, but I can't take this. It was a pleasure to help you." I gently placed the pennies back in her hand. She smiled sweetly and thanked me again. "I'll come by in a few days to see how you're doing. Goodbye, Ms. Nellie!" As I walked away, I looked back, and they were all smiling and waving bye.

From that moment on, I was a joy junkie. I was hooked on that warm, fuzzy feeling you get when you have recognized another person's value, not with words but with a small token of kindness. For me, watching that person start to glow is a moment of real love and pure happiness. My fix was helping wherever and whenever a need came to my attention. I wanted to make that connection with whomever was open to it.

I started dreaming about traveling around the world, helping other people like Ms. Nellie and making a real difference. My friend Linda Craft and I would sit in our seventh-grade class and talk about all the places we were going to go after we graduated from high school. I would run home and tell my mom about our plans, and she would promptly tell me in no uncertain terms that talk like that was unacceptable. My parents were interested in real professions only, not pipedreams. Their main concern was making sure we got good grades in school so we could get scholarships to go to college.

Once a week, my mother would sit on the wooden steps out on the front porch and tell us to line up. It was time to ask each of us what we wanted to be when we grew up. As the line moved forward, I would move backward until, finally, no one was left behind me.

"A fireman, Ma," my older brother Frederick would say, two spots in front of me. "I want to be a fireman in New York City."

A fireman, I thought, *in New York City with all of those high-rises . . . and he gets dizzy standing on an ant mound.*

"What about you?" Mom asked Annette, who was right in front of me. "Have you any idea what you're going to be?" Somehow my little sister managed to come up with a new answer every week.

"I'm going to help doctors. I want to be a nurse."

A nurse. I rolled my eyes in amazement. *Is she serious? Two people had to hold her down the other day for Mom to pull a tiny splinter from her hand.*

My turn could not be put off any longer. Mom looked at me and rolled her eyes. "And Eleze? Have you figured it out yet?"

I stared blankly and shifted my eyes, debating whether or not I should confess. "I—I don't know yet."

Every time, my mother responded the same. "Why do the rest of your sisters and brothers know what they want to be when they grow up, and you don't?"

My head hung lower. "I don't know."

My mom walked away, shaking her head in disgust, and my sisters and brothers looked at me as if I were from another planet. I did not realize it then, but maybe they really did think I was strange. I have always been so different from my siblings, but I have never had a problem with that. I like who I am.

On one normal Sunday morning in April, when I was about sixteen, my pastor bored his eyes into mine. "Child, I can see Him! In you! I can see God in you!" He announced this to the congregation.

While that might not have been the wisest thing to do, for me it was an occasion for pride. It was true that I had been feeling close to God in those days, so I was not at all surprised that the pastor could see it in my face. I had always rested comfortably in the knowledge that the Creator was holding me in His hands. My mother had drummed this knowledge into me all my life, but when I was sixteen, I began to feel His presence more than ever and wanted to share that relationship with everyone.

I know the old Bible-thumping business can be annoying, but really experiencing the presence of God is a taste of perfect love. It is knowing that you are unconditionally loved simply because you exist. It is not about needing fulfillment, nor is it greedy or selfish. It is a generous love, and you cannot help wanting everyone, even perfect strangers, to feel it.

For example, one time my sister Molly, who was attending T.R. Miller High School, told me about a teenage white girl from a well-to-do family in town who had recently been diagnosed with cancer. I knew without a doubt that God could—and would—help her. I felt that God was leading me—a poor black girl—to call her and offer her hope and friendship. Mind you this was the 1960s, in the South.

The girl's name was Susan. When I finally got up the nerve to call, I decided to use my middle name, Denise. Her mother answered the phone.

"Hello," she said. Her voice sounded posh and polite.

"Hi," I replied. "This is Denise. May I speak to Susan, please?"

I heard her put the phone down and call to Susan from far away. It turns out she actually had a friend named Denise.

"Denise! What's up?" Susan said when she picked up the phone.

She sounded too excited. I was nervous to explain who I was and why I was calling. "Hi . . . no, I don't know you personally. I heard about your illness and I was wondering . . . I wanted to pray for you. Is that okay?" My voice was shaky, but I managed to get everything out more eloquently than I expected.

"Yes, please. Go ahead." A shift had occurred in Susan's voice. It was softer than before, and I could hardly hear her.

I prayed aloud right there on the phone, starting off with, "Dear Father, please help Susan." I prayed that she would be healed. I prayed that her family would have the strength to persevere during this trying time. I prayed for her to be strong and believe in the healing power of God. I was nervous and fearful of saying the wrong things, but I didn't. Everything went well.

"Don't worry, Susan," I said when the prayer had ended. "You don't need to worry. God will make sure that you are fine. If you're not busy tonight, you should come by my neighborhood and check out a tent revival we have going on."

There was a pause, and then she finally answered, "Thank you so much. Thank you, I'll definitely try to make it. Thank you for this call, Denise."

I felt good after we talked. I looked for her that night, but she did not come.

I often prayed for Susan, but because we were from very different worlds, it was hard to find out how she was doing. Molly found out that her parents had taken her to one of the biggest hospitals in the area for treatment, and she was going to be okay. I was overjoyed. As the days and months passed, my thoughts of her came less and less.

Although I never spoke to her again, I was overwhelmed by a confusing surge of joy and sorrow when I read that she'd passed away on December 17, 2013—forty-five years later. Her obituary spoke of how she had bravely fought a lifelong battle with cancer. It read, "Her story was not only a story of survival but a story of happy perseverance. Her courage, her faith, and her attitude when fighting her disease will be a legacy for all who knew and loved her."

I often wonder if Susan ever thought about the phone call we shared that day. That was the first time I had ever prayed together with anyone, and I know God heard us because she lived a long, full life after our call.

My main point is that when you have known—I mean intimately known—the embracing presence of God, His love rubs off on you and you can't help seeing everyone through His eyes. Each person becomes a precious treasure that deserves the utmost care.

I guess that's why, when I was sixteen in the late 1960s, the Vietnam War was heavy on my mind. At the time, I didn't really understand what the fighting was all about. I knew people were protesting it. Men were burning their draft cards while others were leaving the country to avoid the draft altogether. What concerned me was that while I was getting a good education to prepare for my future, so many of my brothers would have no future at all. Every other day I read or heard about soldiers getting killed over there. My heart broke, and I mourned every death. These young men weren't much older than I was.

One death hit me particularly hard. Dan Bullock was born in Goldsboro, North Carolina. He lived in North Carolina until he was about twelve, when his mother died and he and his younger sister, Gloria, moved to Brooklyn to live with their father and his wife. There he dreamed of becoming a pilot, a police officer, or a U.S. Marine. When he was fourteen, he altered the date on his birth certificate to December 21, 1949, got processed through the recruiting station, and enlisted in the U.S. Marine Corps. He became a member of Platoon 3039 on Parris Island, graduated from boot camp, and arrived in Vietnam on May 18, 1969. He was assigned as a rifleman and stationed at An Hoa Combat Base. Less than one month later, he was killed by small-arms fire during a North Vietnamese Army night attack while he was making an ammunition run to resupply his beleaguered unit. He was fifteen years old—even younger than I was!

I read about Dan in the newspaper during a senior class field trip stopover in Indiana in the summer of 1969. I and nine other pupils from Southern Normal High School were on our way to Northwestern College in Orange City, Iowa, where we were to take summer college courses. The headline of the paper read, "The youngest soldier to get killed in Vietnam." There was a picture of him in his uniform. He looked so distinguished and handsome. I wondered why he would lie about his age to go to war, especially during the 1960s when there was so much going on in America with the Civil Rights Movement. That was on the front burner at home for most African Americans.

I wondered what kind of life Dan had before he enlisted. I wondered if I could have changed his mind if we'd met and gotten to be friends. I still ask myself these same questions. After reading the article, guilt and sadness consumed me. Here I was safe and sound, while Private Dan Bullock had made the ultimate sacrifice and died for his country. So young, so brave, so proud—what a Marine! He became my hero. Private Bullock was one of 58,266 American soldiers killed in Vietnam—39,966 of whom were twenty-two or younger, and 8,283 of whom were nineteen or younger.

For a long time after the war was over, and all through my twenties, when people asked if I was married, I'd always say, "No, my husband was killed in Vietnam." I felt that with all the men we'd lost in the war, one of them must have been my husband-to-be. I was left with an enduring sadness about how wasteful the world could be with the precious gift of human life. It was this feeling that deeply influenced my decision to fight back and do all I could to show people, especially the poor that they were indeed precious, valued, and loved.

CHAPTER TWO

Chasing Freedom

A lthough today my life's focus is on helping people in need, for years I only vaguely appreciated the joy that comes from giving to others. I did not completely recognize the indignities of everyday human suffering, but in time, with God's patience, I was able to grow beyond myself. Youth, with its many benefits, can at times be a distraction. I needed to mature beyond the myopic vision of girlhood before I could really see the need in the people around me.

When I was a teen, my greatest desire was for nothing but personal freedom—my own independence. With high school graduation approaching and the exhilarating world of college looming just beyond the horizon, I was ready to tackle something new. I'd participated in most of my high school drama productions and showed promise as an actress, so my drama teacher, Mr. Wurpts, recommended me for a drama scholarship at Hope College, a Dutch Reformed Church institution in Holland, Michigan.

For Mom and Dad, college was all about bettering myself and becoming equipped to live the sort of accomplished life a lack of resources had kept them from. College was the path to opportunities that life hadn't afforded them. But to me, college was about the chance to finally be free, to be my own person, to be a "young adult," with everything that implied. While my parents were dreaming of what I could learn and who I could become, I lay awake thinking about the dorm I would live in and the people I would meet. I would have my own key to my own room, and for the first time I would have a roommate who was not related to me.

My best friend from high school, Regina, was also going to Hope, so we became roommates. We were assigned Room 222 in Durfee Hall, which was a great source of amusement to us because of the popular TV show *Room 222*. It was like opening a new cell phone account and being assigned the number 867-5309. Another friend, Joyce Paul, lived across the hall, so I was surrounded by familiar faces.

A little bit of the familiar helped quell some of the anxiety I felt when I discovered that 90 percent of the student body at Hope College was white. It was a daunting realization, but I soon found that the North was different from where I grew up. The color of a person's skin wasn't such a big issue. Wow! What a wonderful awakening! I couldn't wait to see what the world was all about. College was only the beginning.

Of course, as we're all entitled to our own youthful indiscretions, my first worldly college discovery was the boys. On the first day of my psychology class, I looked across the room, and—oh, my goodness!—there he was: one of the prettiest boys I had ever laid eyes on. He looked like Paul McCartney. Oh, yes, I was a Beatles fan. When the white girls were screaming at the top of their lungs and pulling their hair out over a sighting of John, Paul, George, or Ringo, you can most definitely be assured that I was, too.

I was love-struck, enamored, infatuated, and any other word you can think of to signify a girl's first serious crush. His name was Jerry, and I was determined to make him mine. I made a fool of myself chasing him around campus. I wrote him sweet love poems. I invited myself to his table in the dining hall. I called him at all times of the day and night, certain that any moment he would realize we were fated to be together.

Fortunately for me, Jerry was a kind young man with high ethical values, so no matter how hard I threw myself at him, he managed to keep me at arm's length without compromising my dignity. After I pursued the object of my affection for several weeks, the excitement finally wore off. I vowed to take college more seriously and promised myself that I would substitute studying for my crush.

But, despite my vow and my parents' expectations, the more I tried, the more I realized that I had absolutely no interest in spending four years attending classes, writing papers, and studying for exam after exam. In many ways, it was a disheartening epiphany. Here I was, surrounded by people who respected me and went out of their way to make me feel welcome. Hope College was the perfect campus for a small-town girl like me, but I just wasn't interested in a college education. Had I been, Hope would have been exactly the right institution, but I didn't have the desire to pursue this particular life path.

I knew that if I wanted to be happy, I wouldn't be able to please everyone, even my parents, so I made the choice to please myself. I left college, got a job, and adopted a hippie lifestyle (also known as "I had hardly any money, but that was okay because I had even less responsibility"). At the same time, I started dating Leon, a boy I'd met while still in college.

Leon was a tall, dark, good-looking bad-boy type with a Jekyll-and-Hyde personality. Backed by the often-fallible influence of youth, Leon seemed to fulfill everything I thought I wanted in a boyfriend. When it came to men and relationships, I was naïve, and I believed that Leon was "the One." All too soon, I was ready to move our relationship to the next step and indulge in some of his bad-boy activities.

The first thing I tried was smoking cigarettes. I thought it would look sexy for a woman to sit in the car holding a cigarette between her fingers, sipping on a vanilla shake as the wind blew through her hair. Instead, the wind blew the cigarette ash into my afro, and it started to smoke. I panicked, and rather than drinking my vanilla milkshake I ended up wearing it.

Leon was determined to change my good-girl image, so he took me to a small party to meet some of his friends. I was just sitting there enjoying myself when the person sitting next to me handed me a small cigarette. I noticed that everyone else had taken a puff, so I was happy to try it too. When I did I heard a loud pop . . . I immediately fell to the floor and hid under the table. All of a sudden the entire room lit up with laughter. Leon told me that a seed had popped in the joint and made the noise.

I was beginning to think this bad-girl business was getting to be too much work. But even with two strikes against me, I decided to try another method . . . this time with alcohol. With all the cheap wine on the market, I could not understand why we had to have homemade wine. Not being a drinker myself, it only took one glass to make me drunk as a skunk and silly as a goose . . . but I insisted on having several more. Between the bed moving most of the night, my head hurting, and my lips and tongue being numb for three days, I realized that alcohol wasn't for me either. I decided to stop trying to pick up bad habits and let everything happen naturally.

When I took Leon home to meet my folks, they couldn't stomach him. They blamed him for my leaving college and turning to my new "reckless" lifestyle, as they called it. What they didn't understand was that college wasn't for everyone, and it especially wasn't for me. In reality they couldn't accept that I was nineteen, old enough to make my own choices and mistakes, and move in the direction that felt right for my life. And the direction I intended to take my life, at the time, was toward Leon. I announced to my parents that we planned to marry.

Of course, Mom and Dad flipped out at the mention of marriage. Outraged, they threw down the gauntlet of parents everywhere when faced with a daughter's inappropriate boyfriend: "Over our dead bodies will you marry that boy!" But I wasn't fifteen and living at home anymore. With the calm but somewhat condescending tone that only a young girl in love can manage, I responded, "Mom, Dad, I'm nineteen years old now. I'm technically an adult, and that means I can do whatever I want. And what I want is to marry Leon, with or without your permission!"

Before I could even realize the ramifications of what had just come out of my mouth, Dad grabbed his shotgun. Needless to say, Leon and I made a quick exit. We ran down the street with Dad hot on our tails, waving his gun and cussing up a storm.

Once we made our escape, Leon and I went to the courthouse in Brewton, intent on making our nuptial plans official. But karma, or perhaps the guardian angel that watches over us in our parents' stead, was the only thing waiting for us there. When we arrived, we were promptly told that we were not able to obtain a marriage license. The clerk sail that males had to be twenty-one to get married in the state of Alabama.

Immediately, I looked at Leon and thought about how my butt had almost received yet another "bite" from my dad, this time from his shotgun, and all for nothing! But our love would not be deterred. This was only a minor setback, we decided, and one that we would look back on and laugh about when we were old and gray. We quickly hatched another plan. Because the marriage age for men in Michigan was only eighteen, we decided to get married there.

By the time we had driven to Birmingham, I could feel the winter temperature beginning to freeze my passion. My feet felt heavy. When I looked down at them, all I could see were two huge blocks of ice. I knew it wasn't the right time. There were too many obstacles in our way. I asked my intended to take me home before we even hit the state line. We decided to wait for a few years before we tied the knot.

We never did. Instead, Leon and I broke up. Oddly, instead of feeling heartbroken, I felt as if I'd suddenly been freed. I decided it was time to move on and left Brewton again, this time for destinations unknown. I traveled a lot but eventually settled in Atlanta, Georgia. I took on a series of short-term jobs, mostly waitressing, and lived hand to mouth. Atlanta was a tough city to get by in. The pay was poor and the cost of living was high. Everyone I knew was working two or three jobs just to make ends meet, and I was no exception.

As a waitress, I only made about two dollars an hour. The tips weren't good either, though some of the customers were terribly generous with their racist remarks. During a lunch rush one Sunday afternoon, I had the pleasure of serving a customer with a bad haircut and an even worse attitude. When I approached the table to introduce myself and take his order, his murky green eyes traveled from my toes to my head and then back down to my toes. I knew exactly what the look on his face meant, though I didn't have a word for it.

"Hey," I said, "I'm Lisa and I'll be serving y'all. Can I get you something to drink?" My teeth were clenched together and my jaw was locked tight. I forced a smile, determined to humor this customer and keep my mouth shut if he said something intending to set me off. As I was already anticipating the need to bite my tongue, I could only imagine what he was thinking, let alone what he would say aloud.

Then he said it, and despite my preparations, I was caught completely off guard. "Is it true that the mayor of Atlanta is a nigger?" He sneered as he enunciated the last word and then glanced around the table, almost as if he were looking to his peers for some sort of applause or praise.

"Now, I'm not sure if the mayor is one," I replied. "But I can tell you that you, sir, are acting like one. Why don't you look up what that word means so you can prevent yourself from looking like one in the future?" Proud of my quick speech, I turned around and walked away, leaving the table behind me with its patrons' eyes agog and mouths hanging open.

This was the final impetus I needed to find a job with decent pay and customers who would respect me. The summer of 1976 was approaching, and I'd already spent two years in Atlanta. The only independence this city was showing me required very hard work for very little reward. My friend Linda Lowe was in agreement, so we decided to pack our things and try our luck in California. I had managed to sock away a little more than $3,000, and Linda had a Volkswagen Beetle. After two months' preparation, we were ready to travel.

On November 4, 1976, Linda and I set out on the trip of a lifetime. Hitting the road and not knowing what the future had in store made me feel alive again for the first time in months. I learned to drive a stick shift on the journey out west, and we took our time enjoying the scenery and all the people we met along the way. We stopped at yard sales and gift shops, taking breaks at rest areas to nap and read. It took us eight days to complete our move, and when we finally arrived in Los Angeles, California, I fell in love with the place.

Los Angeles was beautiful. The people were friendlier than any I had known before. Compared to this new paradise, the two years spent in Atlanta were a nightmare. Atlanta was a city that had done its best to choke me. In Los Angeles, I could breathe, and I knew that California was the right choice. My old routines of sitting in a classroom or working a nine-to-five nowhere job fell away. I was ready to meet new people and conquer the world. I was only twenty-three years old and ready, willing, and able to move around and take advantage of my youth and lack of commitments. After how things had unfolded in Michigan and Atlanta, I was determined to take my time figuring out the right direction for my future. In the meantime, I decided to live life one day at a time. And, boy, did I have fun, fun, fun!

I had plenty of inspiration for my newfound philosophy. The main thing I loved about California was how people encouraged me to live life beyond its limits and pursue my talents and ambitions. Everyone I met, regardless of how different they seemed from me, was in California for the same reason as me. We were all looking for ourselves, exploring our potential and our dreams. Never have I felt so comfortable and at home in a place that was so completely foreign to me.

Eventually I found myself back in the food industry. I started waiting tables at a small Italian restaurant, but this time it was completely different. The experience I had as a waitress in California couldn't even compare to my old job in Atlanta. I learned about food and cooking, but most importantly, I got along with all the guests. The people weren't close-minded bigots waiting for any opportunity to make a snide remark; they were wonderful, loving people who looked past skin color without hesitation. And get this—they all loved me! I was a natural. I was born to serve. I knew how to make people feel important, which resulted in great tips.

Soon, as a hobby, I started making jewelry. I pursued my new passion whenever I wasn't at the restaurant. My hobby started expanding, and I soon discovered a love of crafting. I made all sorts of jewelry—necklaces, earrings, bracelets—and even started my own line of greeting cards. I was doing well. My life was taking shape, and I was happy. But, like most things on this planet, what goes up must come down.

And I came down—hard.

I hit rock bottom a few months after getting my own place in Los Angeles. When Linda and I first arrived, she met her husband, Robert, and we went our separate ways (though we still kept in touch). I stayed with my Uncle Jimmy. He had a place in the center of the city, and he was kind enough to let me live with him until I got settled. After six months of crashing with Jimmy, I felt comfortable enough to get my own place. I'd saved almost all of my tip money, and my jewelry business was really starting to take off.

However, my ambitions proved to be way too much, way too soon. I was unprepared for the expense of paying my own rent in California and quickly fell behind on payments. Each month I would pay off my rent later and later, and each month my landlord would grow more and more upset. Finally, I was out on the streets. My new "place" became my Gran Torino. I spent more nights than I can remember tossing and turning in the back seat, hoping to get more than four hours' sleep. I was overcome with guilt and shame. My parents knew nothing about my life in Los Angeles, and pride prevented me from returning to my uncle's. I already knew what he would say. "I told you so" were the last words I wanted to hear.

A friend at work told me about a homeless shelter. I decided to check it out and was fortunate that they had a spot available for me. I stayed at the shelter for two months and, by-and-by, was able to save a little money. Slowly, I started to regain my independence. At one point, I picked up a brochure in the community room that had information about the local YWCA. I decided to look into it. I was grateful for the shelter, but felt I needed to move on so someone else who had less than I had could make use of my space.

The YWCA provided housing in a beautiful mansion that had been donated to the city. I inquired about rooming and explained my situation to the women behind the counter. They were most helpful, and once they explained how everything worked, I signed a new lease. Rent was due every week, but I had my own room. Meals were included in the rent fee, so I didn't have to worry about spending money on food. It was a safe, comfortable place for me to stay—a place designed to help women get back on their feet. After seven months at the YWCA, I had found my footing.

The struggles I'd endured made me stronger than before and more appreciative of stability. I became aware of my financial situation and took charge of my spending habits. I realized that constructive spending was the only way I could sustain my independence, and I resolved to stick to a budget. In essence, I'd started growing up. Freedom is a spirit that knows no limits, but I had to set some boundaries if I wanted to maintain a decent lifestyle. I knew that if I didn't, I'd end up in a situation where, in the words of Janice Joplin, *"Freedom's just another word for nothing left to lose."*

Once I'd reestablished myself, I began working various jobs to ensure my new financial stability. I started a savings account and bought a car. My primary job was still waitressing, but I continued making and selling jewelry and greeting cards. I taught myself how to make other things, too: baskets, cakes, and various baked goods. I started fantasizing about becoming my own boss. I knew I could figure out other ways of making money with my own creations.

My new financial practices helped keep the wolf at bay, but money was still tight. All my hours of work provided just enough income to pay my rent, my car note, and to eat. And while I worked hard to save what I could, there was hardly any money left over to put away after monthly expenses were paid. The cost of living was just as high in California as it had been in Georgia. Happily, though, the pay and opportunities for a non-professional were much better.

One of those opportunities presented itself while I was waitressing for a catering company called Tucker's. Tucker's main clients were big law firms in Southern California. The pay was good, the hours were great, and the owner, Fred Tucker, was a wonderful guy to work for. One day while I was on the job, he came in to check on everything. Fred was always up for a chat and loved to stop by and shoot the breeze.

"Good morning, Fred," I smiled. "How are things with you and your wife?" Fred loved talking about Sam, his spouse. It was sweet, actually.

"Sam's doing great," Fred answered. "You know we're expecting the new baby soon. That's why I haven't been stopping by here as often. We're interviewing candidates for a nanny position. It's rather exhausting."

That's when it hit me: I'd be a nanny! I *could* be a nanny. "Well, Fred," I said, testing the waters, "if you still need a nanny, I'd be happy to help you and your wife out and watch the child." I wasn't too sure how he'd react, but I knew I had a chance.

"Actually, Lisa," he said after a minute, "that's a great idea. I know you better than any of those other girls who applied. I already know you're a great worker, and you're honest and kindhearted. You'd be a perfect match. Come by the house later and meet my wife. We'll set up all the details."

That was all it took. Two weeks later, the Tuckers delivered their first child. They named her Tianna. I watched her almost every day. It was the perfect occupation, as being a nanny provided me a little extra cash without interfering with my other work schedules. I could be a nanny during the day and wait tables at night. In between, I still found time to keep my little side businesses going.

This was how I lived for nearly ten years. My own wellbeing was my only concern—my security, my belongings, and my social life. I still hadn't realized that true maturity and freedom come not from looking after one's self, but from looking out for others. However, my conscience would soon come calling, knocking on my head again during the summer of 1987.

That summer my mom had laser eye surgery. I called home to check on her, and when she picked up the phone, she was crying. I could barely make out what she was saying. Mom confessed that the surgery, while improving her eyesight, had also let her see how far her home had fallen into disrepair. She was distressed because now she could see the worn boards on the floor and around the house, the cracked paint on the walls, the ragged carpet, and the soot from the heater on the ceiling. This was the same house that I grew up in, and though it had been renovated a few times, it was still in need of a lot of updates. The floors were weak, the interior of the house was old, and the exterior needed considerable work. It took the surgery to make my mom see her reality, and that broke my heart. Mom knew that Dad had no interest in any kind of home repair. Her children were her only hope of improving her living conditions.

"Mom, I'll be home soon," I said, trying to soothe her. "Don't worry. Just hold on a little longer. I promise you when I get home, I'll work on the house and do whatever I can to make you happy again."

I promised my mom this, but I didn't know whether I could make good on my word. Home renovation required a lot of money. Besides that, I was suffering from carpal tunnel. My years of waitressing and the repetitive motions that work entails had caught up with me. Carpal tunnel is a painful, debilitating injury, and my case was so bad that I had to go on leave from my job at a local hotel and take worker's compensation while I recovered. I didn't know how I was going to help my mother; all I knew was that I had to do something. I couldn't stand to hear her cry.

The following summer, I managed to save up $2,000. I took the money, a few of the nicer items from my home, and some kind household donations from a friend, Greta, and rushed down to Brewton to finally see Mom. As soon as I arrived, I began working on the house.

Although it didn't seem like much, I couldn't believe how far $2,000 went in repairing my parents' home! With that money, I managed to hire carpenters to do the woodwork. They put up new paneling and refinished the kitchen cabinets. While the carpenters worked, I took on the other tasks. I painted and put down new carpet. I hung wallpaper and did what other work I could to revamp my childhood home. The neighborhood started ringing with gossip as people started talking about the grand makeover happening at the Thomas house. Everywhere I went, folks would ask, "Aren't you Bertha and Earlie's daughter, the one from California who's doing the work on their home?"

Four weeks later, the house looked completely different. It still wasn't anywhere near perfect, but I have to admit it looked good. Mom and Dad beamed with pride, regarding their renovated home as if it were a mansion. Boy, did that feel good! Here I was, a little injured waitress from California, and I had made a huge impact in my parents' life. It was one of those moments where I felt the joy that can only come from bringing happiness to others. I understood that though I was not rich in material goods, I could still make a difference with the little I had.

Mom's ultimate response to my home makeover was to begin calling me and asking me to move back to Brewton. My answer always remained that I would do so if God gave me a sign that it was what He wanted for me. But even though God hadn't really given me a sign, the fact that my mom kept asking had started my conscience gnawing at me. Mom needed me. How could I turn my back on her? But I was so happy and secure in Los Angeles. I didn't want to give up the life I'd worked so hard for only to go back to where I came from. Brewton was the place I wanted to break free of, not return to. So I passed the buck to God. If He wanted me to go, He would show me.

He was quiet for six years, but in 1994, out of the blue, He sent me one heck of a sign. On January 17, I was jarred awake by the sound of car horns blaring outside my window. It was four in the morning, and I had been fast asleep for five hours. In my bleary, sleep-addled state, I tried to process what was happening. Lights in my room were flickering on and off, adding to the cacophony outside. Half thinking I was dreaming, I noticed my bed was making its way across my wooden bedroom floor. That shocked me fully awake, and that was when the panic kicked in.

Everything was shaking. The television across the room came unplugged, quivered violently, and pitched viciously from its stand. It hurtled toward me, barely missing me and crashing to the floor. At that moment the lights gave out, plunging me into total darkness. My senses were going crazy trying to pick up any sound, sight, smell—anything that could help me figure out what to do to stay safe. My hand scrabbled under my bed, hoping to find the emergency flashlight I'd stored there, but the shaking had scattered it out of reach.

The world was moving, angry. For those terrifying moments, the earth was unconcerned with human need and human concerns. I could hear crashing and crunching noises coming from all directions outside. Debris was falling to the sidewalks and landing on cars. I could hear neighbors, as scared as I was, screaming. Before this, I'd been in a few small earthquakes. Usually they were nothing more than tremors. But this felt like a monster clawing its way up from underneath the earth, determined to shake the world to pieces.

Despite all the fear and the panic, I remember having one lucid thought: *this was a sign.* Sure, it had been six years since I had asked God to send me a sign as to whether I should return home, but this was it. Once the shaking stopped, I looked up and shouted, "Lord, I asked You for a sign, not a heart attack!"

I was living with a ninety-year-old woman at the time, Mrs. Pointdexter, and she was the first person I thought to check on. If I was scared during this earthquake, I could only imagine how poor Mrs. Pointdexter felt. I got on my knees and proceeded to crawl to her bedroom. When I opened the door, the room was pitch black. I crawled to her bed and gently shook her to see if she was all right. She was snoring and wouldn't wake up.

"Mrs. Pointdexter," I said, speaking softly so as not to scare her. As soon as I spoke she stirred a bit, and I realized that she was still fast asleep. *You have to be kidding me,* I thought. I couldn't believe she had slept through the whole ordeal! But all things considered, it was probably for the best. At least she was peaceful and at ease. She didn't have to suffer any of the trauma from going through the massive quake. I crawled out of the room, all the while thinking, *you lucky stiff.*

Things calmed down considerably once the earthquake stopped, but I could still hear my heart pounding. I crawled to the living room, hoping to find the phone and call my mom. But the phone lines were all down. Unable to contact my family, or really do anything else in the aftermath, I grabbed a bottle of Jack Daniels I'd received for Christmas. I searched the floor, moving among the shaken contents of my room, and unearthed the key to the front door. Opening it, I propped myself against the frame. Luckily, I didn't try to move beyond the doorway, as the front porch had separated from the steps. I watched the neighbors milling around with flashlights, doing their best to comfort each other. I wasn't well acquainted with any of them, so I chose to drink my anxiety away, tipping the contents of the Jack Daniels' bottle into my mouth.

I wanted to quiet my nerves and stop the voices that were screaming in my head. I have to admit my tonic had the desired effect. I was still pretty shaken up and teary-eyed, but the liquor gradually calmed me. I started to relax, feeling myself quietly floating away.

My neighbors, hearing my soft crying, came over to make sure I was okay. They found me crying into my bottle. Yes, it was *my* bottle, and if anyone had tried to take it, they would have had to deal with me. When they saw me, though, they seemed to understand I was making my way through something, mentally reconfiguring the abrupt morning, trying to make sense of its meaning. They were kind enough to shut off the gas to prevent any fires or explosions that could arise. At that point, I wasn't coherent enough to think of common-sense procedures, so I thanked them for their kindness and took another drink.

What bothered me most about this earthquake was that I felt helpless. I was at its mercy and had no power. It was hard for me to deal with this sense of powerlessness, and for the moment the alcohol helped me cope and regain some bit of equilibrium.

It took a few hours for the phone lines to be restored. As soon as they were, I called my mom and sobbed my heart out. There were sounds escaping my mouth, but none of them were really comprehensible.

"Eleze, have you been drinking?" my mother asked, shocked. I couldn't believe she had the nerve to ask me that. The habits of childhood die hard.

"No, I . . . it was . . ." I blurted out, feeling like a truant schoolgirl. I tried to come up with a few words to counter her accusation, but after struggling to even deny the allegation, I knew my case was lost. "I had a little bit to drink," I admitted, and then somewhat defiantly added, "but I'm not drunk!" I decided I would only confess to being slightly toasty. That was understandable; just a little nip to calm my nerves.

"I was watching CNN while the earthquake was happening," my mom said. "It was bad, Eleze. It was real bad. You need to come home."

She had said the words aloud that I'd been thinking since I'd woken up to the disaster. "Yeah, Mom," I mumbled. "I'm coming home."

Mom was thrilled to hear me say it, and she assured me that it was the best thing for me to do. She questioned how I could even have the nerve to stay in a place where the earth shook. After I got off the phone with her, I sat in the doorframe and finished my bottle of whiskey. As daylight finally made its appearance, it witnessed neighbor helping neighbor to cope with the stress of the night. It took a while for the power to come back on, but we all stuck it out and made it through.

Like many things, all that's required to heal a wound is time, and with every passing day after the earthquake my nerves calmed more and more. The urgency to move back home to Alabama lessened and then disappeared altogether. I started settling back into my life in California.

Even though I knew moving back home was the right thing to do, the reality of my decision was difficult for me to accept. I would be moving from a city where my spirit had roamed free for almost twenty years. It was a place where artists and entrepreneurs could meet on the streets, exchange ideas, and share their hopes and dreams. Here, in Los Angeles, I had found people who understood my need for freedom. I could talk to them in a way that I couldn't talk to my parents and friends in Brewton. Here I had found understanding and adventure. There was always some¬thing to do, someone to meet, somewhere to see.

I was scared to leave everything I knew to pursue a path where I had no idea what was waiting for me. I'd already done that in my twenties, and while it had paid off in the end, I couldn't be guaranteed the same success in starting over. Besides, I was getting older, and I was ready to settle down somewhere. I could see that happening in California, but I had trouble picturing that type of future in Brewton. How would I find happiness in a town where little ever happened? Would I be able to find a decent job? And those summers . . . I couldn't even think about those excruciating summer days that

I would have to endure.

Returning to Brewton felt like I was taking the road to nowhere. That was tough. And for all the questions I posed, the only answer I could come up with was uncertainty. That uncertainty brought me back to the days when my mom lined us up and asked what we wanted to be when we grew up. I still didn't have a clue. I was older now, but as I reflected, I wondered if I'd even done any growing up at all. There was still only me to worry about—I hadn't been in a serious relationship in years. I thought marriage was for women who wanted to be controlled. I couldn't imagine living by rules and regulations. My freedom was too important for me to be tied down to one place and have rules to follow. Spontaneity was what made my life worth living, so I decided the single life was best for me.

When God tells you to move on, though, it's best not to test His patience. Four months after the big quake, a strong aftershock hit Los Angeles. I knew that was God's way of nudging me forward. Again, I looked up and shouted, "Okay, okay! Calm down, I'm going, I'm going!" I finally packed up twenty years of California living and, in April 1994, moved back home to Alabama. My car was packed full with my belongings, and I could barely see out the windows as I drove away. After a week of travel, I finally reached Brewton and pulled into that familiar driveway on Fountain Avenue.

But *going home* didn't just mean traveling 2,000-odd miles from Los Angeles to Alabama. It also meant returning to myself, my roots, and who I was meant to become. It meant coming home to true freedom, which, as it turned out, was not the freedom I was anticipating. I thought that returning home as an adult meant that I'd be able to do whatever I pleased, but I was in for a rude awakening. I was to discover that to be truly grown up and truly human meant devoting myself to others rather than always thinking of myself. Freedom from self-interest gives one wings to truly and unconditionally love. And this, I came to discover, is pure joy.

CHAPTER THREE

Sweet Home Alabama

Getting situated in Brewton would take some doing, but I was up to and ready for the challenge. I started looking for a job right away, and I helped my parents by cleaning, cooking, and doing most of the grocery shopping. One of these many trips to the grocery store would end up changing my life forever.

At the checkout there was only one register open, with at least four people with full carts in front of me. Finally, after standing in line for what felt like half an hour, I was next. The elderly woman in front of me was just getting ready to pay for her items, but then a problem arose. She wasn't buying much—her basket was even emptier than mine—but after counting the same coins three times, she finally admitted, with tears in her eyes, that she didn't have enough money. It broke my heart to watch this poor woman count her pennies and nickels again and again. The cashier seemed less than amused by this poor woman holding up her line, and I could see the remark that was dying to escape from her lips.

"Put your change back in your purse," I whispered. "I'll pay for your groceries."

The woman's eyes welled up even more. "Thank you, thank you so much," she said. "God bless you, you are a beautiful soul." She couldn't stop smiling.

The total was only $12.94. I told the cashier to add my groceries to her tab, and I would pay the total. The woman continued on her way, one paper bag in each arm. Once I paid for everything and bagged up my purchases, I hurried out to find her.

"Excuse me," I said when I caught up to her in the parking lot. "Tell me about yourself." Although she seemed surprised by the request, her eyes sparkled at the realization that someone cared.

"There's not much to say," she said shyly as I loaded the groceries into her beat-up station wagon. "My name is Sallie. I am seventy-seven and live alone with my cat, Smokee. Since my husband died a few years back, it's been just me and him."

"Everyone needs a Smokee," I said. We shared a smile. "Do you mind me asking about your living situation?"

"What would you like to know?" I could see the pride welling up in her eyes. As the tears began to fall, I gently touched her elbow to let her know I cared.

"Do you have enough to eat? Is there anything you need?"

"I do the best I can, but it's getting harder and harder to make the dollars stretch. I only get $463 a month. After paying rent and utilities, there is just enough left for my medicine, and that's about it."

"Have you applied for any additional help?"

"Oh, dear, I have applied for everything I can find. I do get seventeen dollars a month in food stamps, but you can imagine how long that lasts." She started to cry again. I knew this woman needed my help.

I put my arm around her and gave a gentle squeeze. "Don't worry. You'll never have to worry about food again." She looked up at me, confused. "Let me take care of your groceries. I'll even throw in some treats for Smokee."

"Why would you help me? You don't even know me."

"It's simple—because it makes me feel good and I care about you. You have worked all your life, and at this point things shouldn't be so hard for you. I promise you, Ms. Sallie, you won't ever have to worry about food again."

Almost immediately, I felt that sensation—that deep, infectious joy that came when my actions helped someone. "Nobody should ever have to worry about food, especially someone like you." I was referring to her age, but I didn't want to sound rude. "I'll be here to ensure, for as long as I can, that the only thoughts you have about food are when you're deciding *what* to eat, not *whether* you can afford to eat."

I felt again like the little girl who had reveled in the joy of giving. Back then, I had understood the struggle to survive in a harsh world the way only someone who had experienced it could, and I had acquired valuable skills. In comparison to the less-fortunate people of Brewton, I had abundant resources. I'd moved back home with $7,000 in my savings, half of which I'd used as a down payment on a house. Plus, after working hard and studying relentlessly, I had passed a certification test and landed a job as an insurance agent. This gave me a flexible schedule and a little money to spare.

With these small resources at my disposal, I started falling back into my old childhood routine of helping out where I could in response to the suffering of those folks whose daily struggles made up the fabric of my life. While at work doing my regular rounds as an agent, I encountered more elderly people who were barely getting by. I was driving through an apartment complex one blistering hot morning when an elderly woman waved me down.

I rolled my window down. "Can I give you a ride?" I asked.

"Actually . . ." she said, looking embarrassed, "I was wondering if I could sell something to you. Would you by any chance be interested in buying a microwave for five dollars? It works great. It's beautiful, too."

"I . . . would need to see it first," I said. She stepped out of the way and motioned for me to park in the spot where she had previously been standing. Leading me to her apartment, number 4A, she turned around and smiled at me reassuringly.

"Why exactly do you want to sell this microwave?" I asked. "Won't you need it?"

"Oh, why yes! Of course I want it, but not as much as I want a sandwich, or as much as I want a little bit of bologna and some bread . . . maybe some bananas, too . . ." I could see her mind getting caught up in her desires as she listed these items. This woman wanted such simple items so badly that she resorted to selling a perfectly good appliance just to be able to afford them.

As soon as we turned the corner into the kitchen, without even seeing the microwave, I said, "I'll take it. Could you get it ready for me? Clean it up while I go to the bank and get the money . . ."

She nodded enthusiastically and escorted me out. Instead of stopping at the bank, I went to the store and bought her two loaves of bread, a bunch of bananas, and two packs of bologna. I knocked on her door thirty minutes later, and when she saw what I had in my hands, the expression on her face was priceless.

I handed her the bags and assured her that she would never go hungry again. I handed her my phone number and a twenty-dollar bill and gave her a big hug. Her name was Mary Alice, but I called her my "3-B Girl" because she always asked for bread, bologna, and bananas.

There were too many others like her in my community. Some were simply lacking the motivation to cook for themselves. Others didn't have the money to buy the food they needed. A few were in their nineties, one was legally blind, and others were in wheelchairs. They couldn't be eating healthy, and I had to do something about it.

I met a woman named Ms. Nelson on my insurance route, and she directed me to more people in need. In February 1995, I started a free breakfast delivery service for the elderly. I began waking up earlier and earlier every morning to prepare twenty-nine hot breakfasts in my own kitchen. I stopped at a nearby fast-food restaurant to pick up twenty-nine coffees, and then I delivered these meals door-to-door to hungry seniors, who always welcomed me with love.

At each of my delivery stops, I would make sure that they had enough food to last the rest of the day. It didn't take long for word to spread. The number of people calling and asking for help started to shoot through the roof. It was only by the grace of God that I was able to aid them for as long as they needed me. But all of this came to a screeching halt in October 1995, when my life nearly came to a sudden end.

It had been a while since I'd experienced a natural disaster other than an earthquake, so it caught me by surprise when I found everyone was in a frenzied state of preparation for a hurricane. People were shopping with frantic urgency for food and emergency supplies. As the hurricane came closer, storeowners closed their doors early and boarded up their windows. For some reason, though, I just didn't take the threat of Hurricane Opal that seriously. I got off work, went home, cooked some supper, and sat down to relax and watch TV. The most I did as a precaution was set up candles around the house in case the power went out.

Once night fell and the lights went out, I realized I'd made a terrible mistake. I looked out my window, hoping to see some sign of comfort, but all I saw was complete darkness. It seemed that all of my neighbors had left, and the power was out around the neighborhood. I felt completely alone. I started reminiscing about my childhood. When there was a hurricane or tornado warning, we would all get on the back of Dad's truck and head for shelter to Booker T. Washington School. Although it was a dangerous time, it was always wonderful for us kids because we got to live like one big family with the other parents and children who showed up. Sometimes we spent most of the night there, and other times just a few hours, but we all enjoyed it.

My mom and sister Jane kept calling me that night to tell me that I was crazy to stay by myself. They said I should leave my house and join them before conditions got any worse. At that point, however, the weather was terrible and by no means safe to drive in. I was terrified, and my mother and sister were only making matters worse.

I held up pretty well until around 7:30 PM, when the wind started to pick up speed. I could feel the entire house shaking, and it reminded me of the earthquake I'd been in the year before. It felt like I was caught between two terrible disasters. I started calling it a "hurriquake." Finally, my fear got the best of me. I was too scared to stay by myself, and, figuring it was now or never, I decided to make a move. I called my mom to tell her I was on my way, stepped out my front door, and struggled to make my way to my little Geo Metro.

The gusts of wind were so strong. I thanked God I had some meat on my bones so I wouldn't get blown away. The door of the car blew open as soon as I pulled on the handle, and I hopped inside and pulled against the wind to slam it shut. I sat there for a minute, watching the weather continue to unfold, and started regretting my decision to leave. But I hated the idea of going back into a dark house even more, so I buckled up my seatbelt, backed out my driveway, and started slowly driving toward Highway 31 South.

To my surprise, aside from the occasional gust of wind that pushed my car to the side of the road, the drive went relatively smoothly. I could drive no faster than 25 MPH due to the poor visibility, but I was making good time. I was probably five minutes away from my destination when I drove over a small hill. As I reached the top, I saw something I'd failed to see from the bottom: a huge fallen oak tree was blocking the entire width of the road. I couldn't avoid it; my car was inevitably traveling toward its own demise. As I headed closer and closer to the tree, I said to myself, *I'm going to die. I am going to hit this tree, and I am going to die.*

However, instead of being overcome with panic or fear, I felt a calming sensation envelope my entire body. I shut my eyes and squeezed the wheel so tightly that I could feel the beads of sweat getting captured between my palm and the leather. I immediately began to see my entire life flash through my mind like a racecar. First I saw my family, and I thought about how they would react after receiving the news I'd died in a car accident. Then I remembered the $10,000 life insurance check I had in the car, which I was supposed to deliver to a client. Then, BAM! My car smashed into the large oak with a sickening crunch.

My seatbelt hugged my ribcage and snapped me back into my seat. Before I knew it, it was over. My eyes were still shut; I thought I was dead. But as the seconds passed, and I slowly started to open my eyes, I realized I was still alive. "Cool," was the only word that came out of my mouth.

When I got out of the car, I turned around and saw a bright light coming toward me. *Omigosh!* I thought. *I am dead after all! I am going into the light!* In my disoriented state, I began running toward "the light," only to discover that it actually belonged to a group of Good Samaritans from a nearby church. They had heard the crash and, in spite of the hurricane, had decided to come and see if they could help. To my disbelief—and I'm sure to everyone else's—I only had a small cut on my forearm.

"I . . . I'm okay," I said. "Really, I'm okay!" The Good Samaritans insisted on calling an ambulance to pick me up, and I insisted that I didn't need one. Twenty minutes later, I was strapped to a stretcher and taken to the emergency room. I only needed four stitches. I was truly blessed! When they later called my family to tell them about the accident, my mom and sister felt so guilty for asking me to leave and come to them. But they were eternally grateful that I was okay.

Unfortunately, I couldn't say the same for my car. My poor little Geo Metro was totaled. The insurance company told me my car had hit the tree trunk below the branches, and that if I had crashed into the branches, I would have been killed. I didn't realize how good God had been to me until a few days passed and the shape of the seatbelt appeared across my chest, red and bruised.

In my mind, God had spared me for a purpose, but what was it? I still couldn't figure out why God continued to spare my life and present me with chances to make a difference in the world. But in the meantime, I preoccupied myself with the newfound value I had placed on life. It took me nearly being killed in a car accident to really understand how precious and fragile life is. I was extremely thankful for all that I had, and I knew this applied to everyone else around me. Far too many folks, who were as dear to God as me, had too little to be thankful for.

The awareness that followed the "hurriquake" inspired me to double my efforts to help all those precious and vulnerable people in need. First, I expanded the area in which I operated. I had heard there was a plethora of poor folks in nearby rural areas who didn't have enough food, but I needed a larger vehicle to be able to transport groceries and supplies to the countryside. I had borrowed my dad's little Nissan truck, but it was too tiny for the task.

"God, please show me a way," I prayed. "What should I do?"

About a week later, my sister Shirley called. "Hey, Lisa," she said. "Since your car was totaled in the accident, you need a vehicle, right?"

I made a kind of "uh-huh" noise into the mouthpiece. I didn't know what to say.

"Would you like to buy my van? It's about ten years old, but it only has 70,000 miles on it."

"Yes! Yes, absolutely." I knew that her van would be perfect for the job I was trying to do. "How much are you going to charge your poor, dear sister?" I asked, trying to use the fact that we were family to get her to cut me a break.

"How does $400 sound?" It sounded as if that was the price she was going to ask for anyway, but that was fine. Four hundred dollars was way cheaper than any price I'd get if I tried to go out and find a used vehicle.

"I'll take it." God had answered my prayer. He always gave me confirmation when I was doing something He wanted me to do.

About a week later, I turned the van into a well-stocked "rolling store." I assembled homemade shelves to put in the back and filled them with groceries from Spam to homemade preserves. Store coupons made the food more affordable, and soon I was buying a dozen newspapers a week just to get enough coupons to keep up with the demand. Grocery stores in Florida were the most promising, as they continued doubling and even tripling their coupons. The trip to Florida was only about forty-five minutes away, so my friend Ruby and I drove there several times a week. Shopping for food wasn't my favorite thing to do, but using store coupons made it more exciting. I was always curious to see how much I could save.

My rural route extended into two counties. I usually preferred having someone travel with me, and we would often visit with folks who'd been referred to us or who had asked for help. Sometimes, though, we'd approach households uninvited and ask if they needed anything. The responses were generally the same.

"Yes, we *could* use a few groceries . . ." That was my cue to have them step outside and follow me to the rolling store. I'd open up the doors and show them the shelves lining the interior of the van. "Feel free to take whatever you need," I would say, "but please only take things that you will actually use."

Some folks were too proud or embarrassed to admit they needed help, so it usually took a bit of convincing. We could often judge their need by their living conditions. I witnessed some of the most heart-wrenching living situations when I was out in the van. Some people's floors were so weak that I could hardly walk on them. Others were somehow living without electricity. Old Ms. Ruthie, a seventy-eight-year-old mother of nine grown children, didn't even have running water.

Ms. Ruthie's husband had passed away a few years before, and she was living in a deteriorating family home off a dirt road near a hunting area. During hunting season, Ms. Ruthie was constantly jumping out of her skin from the sound of the relentless gunfire. Because she didn't have any running water in her house, she had to endure a horrible stench. Her granddaughter usually stayed with her just to keep her company. Every day, the two of them would haul dozens of milk containers full of water into her home to wash with and flush the toilet. They would cook meals on a single hotplate that was perfectly balanced on top of a broken stove.

Sadly, Ms. Ruthie's lack of water wasn't only due to her being unable to pay the water bill—the pipes under her house had burst. She had little money, so she couldn't afford to rent another place or repair the pipes. After seeing Ms. Ruthie's house, I reported her case to a welfare agency. Eventually, they got her into a home for senior citizens.

During one of our unsolicited visits, we met a couple in their eighties living on a back-country road. The old, unpainted wooden house was in shambles. At first we thought the house was abandoned, but as we pulled into the yard, we could see an elderly couple sitting on the porch. "Hi there, my name's Lisa," I said, introducing myself as I shut the car door behind me. "My friend Ruby and I are going around the community and offering our services. Do you need groceries or anything of the sort?"

In unison, the couple answered with a resounding "yes."

It was a hot summer day, so we offered them a bottle of cold water. They gulped that water down as if they'd just emerged from the desert! The wife had to use a walker, so her husband came down the driveway to check out what we had in the van. He selected some groceries, but he didn't really touch too much. I noticed that he was only taking non-perishable items, even though we had a cooler full of lunchmeats, hot dogs, smoked sausage, and bacon. After he made his selection, Ruby and I bagged the groceries and helped carry them inside. The house was cluttered with personal items, the curtains were in tatters, and the floors were beyond weak. When we got to

the kitchen we noticed there was no refrigerator, which explained his prefer-
ence for non-perishable foods.

"You don't have a fridge?" I asked.

"No, ma'am," he said politely. "Haven't had one in quite some time."

"We will see what we can do about that," I said, trying to offer them
hope along with their groceries.

"You've done so much already," the woman said. "We are very grateful."

We put away the groceries and said our goodbyes. The next day, we took
them a cooler full of ice. It was far too hot for them to be without a fridge.
After our initial visit, we visited them twice a week for six months, each time
delivering food and ice. They eventually went to live with relatives.

Eighty-four-year-old Ms. Pugh sometimes lay on the floor all night in
her big old house, her four dogs barking as she called for help. Her little face
was shiny and dirty, and her clothes and body were unwashed. I always felt
grateful on the days she allowed me to take her dirty clothes home to wash.
I'd been bringing food to her for a few months when her family finally decided that their last resort was to put her in a nursing home.

I visited her a few weeks after she'd moved in to give her some time to
adjust. When I got there, I saw the way her face lit up. She was clean, and
her hair was neatly brushed and as white as snow. Everything was glowing,
except her eyes. Those big brown eyes welled with tears when she saw me.
All that she really wanted was to be at home with her beloved dogs and for
someone—anyone—to be there for her when she cried out for help. Helpless
and hopeless over her plight, I felt defeated. I knew she was in the best place
for her well-being, but I wished that she could be happy. I couldn't understand why she couldn't have both.

I could go on and on with examples of people we encountered on a daily basis who were in dire need of standard goods. They were all wonderful,
hardworking people who had tried their hardest to get by and support themselves. Unfortunately, their best just had not been enough for them to get by
in their old age, and they had no strength left to do anything about it. There
were no IRAs, Fannie Maes, or savings accounts for them to fall back on. All
they had were their monthly checks.

Even though I did all I could, I lay awake on the night of October 24,
1997, wondering if I was making a difference. I asked God for guidance. What
happened next actually occurred a few hours later, but it felt like it happened
immediately. At three o'clock in the morning, a 4.8 earthquake hit Brewton.

Talk about déjà vu. There I was, wide-eyed with no sleep in sight during the early morning hours in Alabama, not California, when my bed started to shake. I sat up in disbelief. "It can't be an earthquake," I said, but as the shaking continued I decided to jump out of bed and stand under the doorway as a safety precaution. I was too shocked to be really scared. I decided to call the police department and see what was going on, but the lines were busy. So I called my mom, knowing that she would have the answers and comfort that I needed. Instead, she answered the phone frantically, yelling about the house shaking. She woke Dad and told him to get the gun, thinking the prisoner who had escaped from the road gang that day was trying to break into the house through the floor boards.

I said, "oooooooooooooookay." I assured her that it was an earthquake, that it was over, and that she could go back to sleep. After I got off the phone, I couldn't help but have a big laugh at what she'd said. I called another friend and asked if she had felt the earthquake. "No," she said. "Wait, was that what that was? I had just opened the refrigerator and started eating a chicken leg when it hit . . . I thought somebody was trying to break into the house. I threw that chicken leg in the air and went to my bedroom and locked the door." I assured her she was safe, hung up, and had another big laugh.

I called two more people that night. One thought a bunch of wild dogs had gotten into her house and were fighting under her bed. Another thought her dresser was possessed and trying to attack her. I was in stitches. The next day, the city was abuzz talking about the earthquake. All I could think was, *you can run, but you can't hide.* An earthquake was a very rare and very big deal in Brewton.

I was learning with each passing day that it wasn't just food that people needed. Soon, I started getting phone calls from people asking for appliances. Everything from stoves and refrigerators to air conditioners and heaters were in high demand. We always found a way to help with what we could, but it was becoming increasingly clear that my finances could not support all the demands. The only reasonable thing I could help with was food, and this was with the aid of those amazing coupons.

A speed bump slowly began to form in my path to helping others. The number of food coupons available in the papers was decreasing, which made it more difficult for me to meet my obligations. I needed a way to bring in some cash—fast. So my friend Vanessa suggested that I make salads to sell to women in the offices around town. I loved the idea! I had learned how to cook at my waitressing jobs in L.A., and since then I had loved cooking and preparing meals for others to enjoy. Salads were beautiful and easy to make. I knew I wasn't looking for anything big—I just needed to sell about twenty salads a day. With the money that would bring, I'd be able to help supply the basics to those who depended on me.

It worked like a charm. In fact, it worked so well that in 1998 I quit my job as an insurance agent and started my own catering business. I worked from home and delivered food to workers at job sites. However, as much as I tried, the number of impoverished people I was helping only increased, and soon the profit I was making from the catering business wasn't enough to cover the expenses. It was time to open up my own restaurant. My doors would be open to anyone who wanted a nice, hot meal—whether they could pay or not.

In 2000, I rented a building across from a railroad track in a spot that would attract those in need. It was in an area we referred to as "the bottom." The building was in such disrepair that the owner forgave my first six months of rent to give me time to fix it up before opening. I was able to pay for the repairs with an income tax refund, and the building ended up looking quite respectable. My sister Annette donated five tables, with four chairs each. I decided to name the restaurant "Drexel and Honeybee's." It was a name I'd come up with in California when I had dreams of opening my own ice cream shop. Even though those dreams never came to fruition, I figured the name didn't have to go to waste. Inside the new restaurant was a small salad bar and a hot bar where I could serve home-cooked Southern dishes. Some of the favorites were collard greens, macaroni and cheese, and cornbread dressing.

The restaurant took off. I only charged three dollars a meal, and those who were in desperate need received their meals on the house. I only made about $100 a day. All the money went directly to bills, supplies, and a small income for those who worked with me. The true payment for us wasn't the cash; it was the satisfaction of helping those who were in need. A cycle formed in which the more people I helped the better I felt, and the better I felt the happier I was.

Within a few weeks of opening, I received a letter from the manager of a local senior citizens complex. In the note she asked each restaurant in Brewton to bid for a job preparing hot meals for about twenty-five elderly people who were either unable to make meals for themselves or did not have the means to purchase food. I immediately called her and offered my services for free. The manager was in awe. Apparently, we were the only restaurant that had responded.

Five days a week, I would prepare twenty-five meals, and the manager would pick them up at the restaurant and deliver them. As time passed, more people heard about the free meals, and soon the number climbed to twenty-eight a day. However, if I wanted to continue doing everything, I was going to have to find a way to buy the groceries I needed at lower prices. When word spread, a local pastor reached out and told me about the Bay Area Food Bank in Mobile, Alabama. I wasn't familiar with how food banks operated, so I called them.

Apparently, in order to receive their assistance, I had to be a non-profit organization or a church. I tried to explain my position, and though they were sympathetic, they were unable to do anything for me. "What can I do?" I asked. I sounded helpless. I needed their help, but I had no idea how to go about setting up a non-profit organization.

"You can try contacting Church of Saints. They might be able to donate some food to you while you figure everything out." I contacted the church, and they agreed to sell me the food I needed. But this was only a temporary fix—I needed to form a non-profit organization. Once I'd put my mind to it, I started dreaming big. I was going to establish Brewton's first full-time food bank and hot meal delivery service. I would call my non-profit organization "Carlisa" in remembrance of a close friend, Moses Carstarphen, who had been killed in a car accident in August 2000. I took the first three letters of his last name and added them to the beginning of my name, Lisa.

I had no idea how to set up a non-profit organization, so I went online to research the process. Low and behold, I found out it could cost up to $1,500 just to have a lawyer do all the paperwork! I realized I would have to do as much of the paperwork and preparation as I could myself. I went online, printed the forms I needed, and spent a few hair-pulling days filling them out. A local lawyer named Melinda Maddox volunteered to look over the forms before I submitted them to the IRS, and my application was finally ready to go in early March 2002. Just a few weeks later, I received my letter of approval. After a small payment of $150, Carlisa, Inc. was now a 501c3 non-profit organization. Our mission statement was, *"We feed the need."*

So here I was in Brewton, but still living exactly as I had in California—working several jobs and roaming free. This time, however, my primary job wasn't serving tables in someone else's restaurant in the hope of getting big tips. I had finally realized my dream of becoming my own boss, and I was serving food to those who could give nothing in return except their infectious joy. That was far more rewarding than any amount of money a paying customer might have tipped me. The small sacrifice of my L.A. lifestyle had turned out to be no sacrifice at all. I had lost nothing, and in turn I had gained myself. I was home free.

Looking back, I don't think I would ever have found such happiness in Los Angeles—not because of the city itself, but because it wasn't home. The people in the City of Angels were friendly, exciting, and inspiring, but they weren't *my* people. I had to come home to remember that true freedom and joy is found only in loving unreservedly. I could only experience that depth of love among people I knew as well as I knew myself—those with whom I was deeply connected through shared experiences, shared reference points, and shared struggles. That's how it was with my people in Brewton. I could love them with all my heart because they were the ground of my being. To this day, I thank God that He gently—and sometimes not so gently—prompted me to come home.

CHAPTER FOUR

Where There's a Will . . .

With the way life was going, it felt like I was floating in seventh heaven. But in the words of William Shakespeare, *"The course of true love never did run smooth."* Our excitement about the food bank's new status was short-lived. Although we were now officially in action as a non-profit, that designation came with a few caveats, one of which threatened to derail the project before it could get fully off the ground.

Evidently, we were not allowed to store or cook food purchased from the food bank in the restaurant's kitchen. According to regulations, food banks can't sell to restaurants—they can only sell to non-profit organizations or churches, collecting what's called an "administrative fee." Now that we were an "official" food bank, we could only use the organization's food for the purpose of directly benefiting people in need. The bottom line was that we needed a separate kitchen.

It was a discouraging blow, but when driven by the love of God and neighbor, one can always find a way. Problems are mountains, and like Sir Edmund Hillary said, *"Mountains are meant to be climbed."* The food bank was running out of time. A solution had to be found, and quickly. It was crucial that the restaurant remain open to the public so that the food bank still had a source of income. But those funds were already pledged to the food bank's general operation. There wasn't enough money to spare to rent a separate kitchen.

As always in impossible situations, I turned to the person I knew best— God. I asked Him to give me some insight and guide me in the right direction. Like a shining star from heaven, the solution came to me in the middle of the night. I would build a kitchen behind my own home. It was perfect! The food bank wouldn't have to pay extra rent, and the kitchen would be conveniently located behind my house. I called up the health department and arranged a meeting. The health inspectors visited the property and provided me with a list of what I would need to do to ensure that the food bank's new kitchen was up to code.

We were soon ready to proceed with the project and desperate to acquire building materials. We asked some local building supply companies to donate lumber and hardware, but no one stepped up. The food bank didn't even have the funds to put down a foundation. I wasn't in much of a financial position to help, as I only had five dollars to my name. I was feeling hopeless.

A short time later, a customer from Atlanta visited the restaurant. I saw her admiring the artwork decorating the restaurant's walls. Spotting me, she crooked her finger in my direction. "Excuse me, miss," she said. "Do you know anything about these paintings? I'd love to find out more about the artist. Where did you find these?"

I smiled. "Actually, I . . . uh . . . I painted those." The woman seemed a bit confused, so I explained. "I went through a bit of a phase a few years ago. I was painting everything."

The woman looked at me, and then back at the art. "Well, I love them! I'm quite the collector of folk art. Would you, by any chance, be willing to part with these?" Seeing my hesitation, the woman pressed on. "Would $800 be enough to convince you?"

Perplexed, I just stared at her. These were the last pieces in my collection, but $800 sure sounded tempting. Before I realized I'd even made my decision, I blurted out, "Yes! Yes, you can have them all. Eight hundred sounds very fair. Thank you so much! I'm glad you like them."

"Great," the woman responded with a smile. The deal was struck. "Whom should I make this check out to?"

I knew the paintings could have been sold separately for a higher profit, but this was a sure sale, and the proceeds would provide a great start for the food bank's kitchen. We hired a carpenter to lay the foundation, but just that small start bled our funds dry. We cast about for alternate solutions, and a local carpenter named Earl, a blessing if ever there was one, offered to work on the building in his spare time, free of charge. I did what I could to help Earl as he patiently taught me the ropes of the construction business. So, not only was Earl getting the food bank's kitchen built, but he was also teaching me a new trade! In two weeks, the ceiling, walls, and roof were in place. Additional help came from angels right here on earth who helped hook up the electricity, water lines, and put the building's steps in place.

Now that the kitchen was built, it needed to be equipped. Our bare kitchen lacked nearly everything from appliances to pots and pans to even a sink. A local business answered one need before I could even ask by donating a refrigerator to the cause—and a brand new one at that! My friend Annie also generously donated a sink. Inspired by the response from the community, I joined in the giving, pulling out a few things from my own kitchen: a stove, some pots and pans, cutlery, and a worktable. Our little kitchen was only big enough to cook in, so I ended up storing the provisions in my living room, a largely unused space that suited that purpose perfectly.

With the kitchen fully functional, all that was left was for us to pass our health inspection. A few days later, the inspectors from the health department returned, and we passed. The food bank followed suit by passing an inspection of its own, and just like that I was ready to place my first order.

Now that the kitchen was up and running, I knew I had to make a choice. I simply didn't have the time or the resources to run both the new kitchen and the restaurant. Given the community response and help I'd received in getting the food bank kitchen working, I knew I had to put my trust in God and commit to the path He was taking me down. I closed the restaurant.

Although I felt pretty down about doing this, my choice turned out to be the right one. Someone sent word about our cause to the *Mobile Press Register*, a newspaper in Mobile, Alabama. Renee Busby, a columnist for the paper, got wind of a potential story for their "Volunteer Profile" section and made a trip to Brewton. She wrote a full-page segment about feeding the hungry that prominently featured the food bank.

The response to the article was overwhelming. The morning after the article ran, Pat Smith, a Brewton local, called and asked me to meet her at a local grocery store. When I got there, I was surprised to find her standing beside a shopping cart filled with bags. She had heard about the food bank and, being more than eager to help out, loaded my car with the chicken she'd purchased at the store. Doug Mitchell also called and volunteered his computer know-how to create a bi-monthly newsletter to send out to donors and potential donors to keep them informed of our progress. The youth department from St. Stephens Episcopal Church donated their time and raised more than $400 to help Carlisa.

The newspaper article, in turn, prompted WKRG-TV from Mobile to come out and do an interview with us. Once the news story aired, donations started pouring in from all over Alabama. Two separate Sunday school classes from Florida chose to make Carlisa, Inc. their community project. Not long after that, Sue Straughn from WEAR-TV in Pensacola, Florida, did a third news story on our project. Their entire segment called *Angels in Our Midst* covered the food bank and its mission. After that segment aired, the response doubled. Church groups volunteered their time, adding to our food box and making deliveries. Two local foundations chipped in with monetary donations. Suddenly the food bank had sufficient resources to feed the hungry.

It felt as if Jesus had done with our small offerings the same as He'd done when He fed 5,000 people with five loaves of bread and two fish. I had given up the restaurant, Earl had given up his free time, Annie had given up her sink, and countless others had dedicated their resources to our project. In response, God had increased it 5,000 fold! But the interviews didn't stop with *Angels in Our Midst*. The community interest in the food bank continued, so a short while later Debbie Williams from WSFA in Montgomery, Alabama, came down to Brewton and followed me around for a day in the rolling store. I've included a transcript of that interview below.

Anchor: It's not often we find out what we're supposed to do in life at a young age. It took Lisa Thomas a while to figure it out, too. But now she thinks she knows what it is, and for the last three years it's been her mission. Debbie Williams caught up with her out along County Road 12.

Debbie Williams: They just don't seem to make 'em like Lisa Thomas anymore. She's been called a "guardian angel."

Lisa [in the background]: Hey, Mr. Smith. How you doin'? Miss Kathleen? You doing all right today?

Debbie Williams: For these folks, she is.

Food Bank Patron: Old Grandma is hobbling. I don't know what I'd do if it wasn't for this youngin' feeding me. I don't know what I would do without her. I just love her.

Debbie Williams: Lisa Thomas feeds the hungry.

Lisa: We have rice with chicken, blueberry cobbler, and green beans.

Debbie Williams: And she does it all for free.

Lisa: Everything is free. Everything is free.

Debbie Williams: Growing up in Brewton, she knows the city well, but she always felt a little lost on these streets, searching.

Lisa: Just really never had a solid foundation [she says between stops], and even like five years ago, I went, "Well, Lisa, what do you want to be when you grow up?" Well, I have grown up, 'cause this is what I want to be.

Food Bank Patron: My goodness, she has the best meals.

Debbie Williams: She knows her clients like they were a part of the family.

Lisa: He usually gets stuff off the van [she says of a patron]. What about some corn flakes, peanut butter, apple juice [offering choices]? We don't turn anybody away . . . if they are old or disabled. Course, if they got money, most of them already got people doing it. So, if they call you, they need it.

Debbie Williams: As much as her clients need her, Lisa Thomas needs them just as much. That old adage, "it's better to give than receive"—Lisa Thomas lives that every day.

Lisa: If you throw out positive seeds, they'll multiply and come back.

Debbie Williams: It's a philosophy that makes the world a better place, and it's certainly working for Lisa Thomas. In Brewton, Debbie Williams, along with photojournalist Frank Miles, somewhere out along County Road 12.

All the donations pouring in provided us with the opportunity to reach out to more people in need—and, sadly, there was a constant supply of those in need. Local agencies began sending referrals to Carlisa, Inc. The referrals usually fell into one of two groups. The first consisted of the elderly who didn't qualify for food stamps or were getting too few, as well as families who had applied for benefits but hadn't started receiving them yet.

The second group consisted of the "working poor," or those who worked but didn't make enough to sustain their families. Unfortunately, because they were working, this also meant that they made too much money to get help from any government agency. These were people who were just one paycheck away from disaster. Given the precariousness of my own situation, it was these people whom I held dearest to my heart.

Not only did I relate to the working poor because I was one of them, but I also felt indebted to them. They maintain the roads we drive. Our parks and streets are clean because of them. When we travel, our hotels and motels are clean and comfortable because of them. They wait on us in our favorite restaurants. We all live better lives because of the working poor.

It's terribly unfair that they are so responsible for our high quality of living and yet struggle so mightily with their own quality of life. Most live paycheck to paycheck, which makes it difficult for them to set aside any sort of savings that they can access once they get older. Later, they fall into the first group of people—the elderly poor. Once retired, they often can barely feed themselves, let alone pay for medicine and other needs. These people, more than any other, deserve our compassion. More importantly, they deserve our gratitude.

Although it gave me great joy in knowing that the food bank was easing their burden a bit, it still wasn't enough. Daily, we were surrounded by people in need, and not just for food. People were suffering. We had to do more.

I met a man named Kelly. During his early fifties, Kelly was diagnosed with terminal pancreatic cancer, and his doctors estimated that he had only six months left to live. The oncologist prescribed an aggressive course of treatment—one that required Kelly to travel more than 100 miles several days a week. Traveling that distance so frequently required a great monetary sacrifice. At the time, gas prices were higher than they'd ever been. And, of course, because of his condition, Kelly could no longer work and had limited income. When we heard Kelly's story, we decided Carlisa, Inc. would expand its reach. Through the power of God, we managed to stretch our already-tight budget and help Kelly, and others like him, get to their treatments.

Helping Kelly inspired us to help in other ways. A worker from the local nursing home took it on herself to find help for one of their residents. The elderly woman's teeth were in terrible condition, and she lived in such excruciating pain that she could hardly eat. Her teeth needed to be pulled immediately, but the woman couldn't afford the dentist's fee for the extraction, and the dentist wouldn't perform the procedure without being paid in advance. The worker couldn't stand to see the woman in such agony, so she approached Carlisa, Inc., hoping to find a way to offset the cost of the dental procedure. We obliged, offering what financial help we could. The elderly woman's teeth were removed, which drastically reduced her pain and dramatically improved her quality of life.

Of course, sometimes the help that was needed wasn't financial. Sometimes, just being there was what mattered. Mrs. Murphy, at the age of eighty-two, was no longer able to manage trips to the grocery store or prepare her own meals. She had a son, but because he was unable (or unwilling) to recognize his mother's advancing age, or because he was simply immature, he didn't take the time to make sure his mother was eating. The food bank had received several reports that Mrs. Murphy was desperately in need of groceries. So we decided to act.

On a makeshift reconnaissance mission, I went directly to Mrs. Murphy's home, intent on finding out what her favorite foods were. I knocked lightly on the green wooden door four times. Before I could knock for a fifth, from inside a loud-voiced Mrs. Murphy yelled, "COME IN!" I walked in and promptly met Mrs. Murphy. I was shocked by her appearance. She was extremely frail, a ghostly apparition with long white hair and a long white gown trailing behind her.

"Hi, Mrs. Murphy," I began congenially. She didn't seem pleased to see me, so I used as friendly a tone as possible. "I just came by to check on you and make sure you were okay. May I ask what you've had to eat today?"

Mrs. Murphy eyed me suspiciously. "I don't remember what I've eaten," she announced defiantly. Just as quickly she added, defensively, "I'm not hungry, though."

I knew that the hunger kit in my car contained a can of Vienna sausages and some crackers. I went back outside to grab them. When I returned, Mrs. Murphy seemed more confused by my presence than angry. Pressing what I hoped would be an advantage, I extended my hand and held my offerings out to her. "I've got some snacks here I'd like for you to eat," I said. "Do you think you could do that? Even if it's just a few crackers, you need to eat."

Mrs. Murphy made me wait a few seconds before she finally met my hand with her own. Despite her contention that she wasn't hungry, she ate most of the food. I was relieved to find that she at least had milk and cereal in her kitchen. Her son was living with her at the time, so I asked him to make sure she had breakfast before he went to work the next morning. I left the pair, promising that I would stop by the next day with lunch. Sadly, though, my visit the following afternoon found a hungry Mrs. Murphy. Her son had left for the day without even pouring his mother a bowl of cereal. Instead of relying on the son, Mrs. Murphy became a regular on the food bank's delivery schedule. We tended to her every day until she passed away a few years later.

In my mind, I wanted to believe that people like Mrs. Murphy's son were an exception. I liked to think that if everyone knew how serious hunger was, scores of people would come forward to help. But how could that message best be spread?

I turned to God yet again and asked Him to give me direction. "God," I said, "what should be done to make people see and believe that others around them are going hungry? What can I do to move people into action?" A few seconds later, the answer rose up from my center and formed into a crystal-clear message in my mind. I would walk to Montgomery, Alabama, and deliver a letter to Governor Bob Riley, informing him of the plight of the state's hungry and poor.

My eyes widened, and I began coughing. Puzzled and shocked, I looked around the room. Maybe God was talking to someone else. Or maybe it wasn't God talking to me at all. Maybe it was "the other one." I mean, really? Did God know how far that was? He certainly wouldn't ask me to do that. He knew better! The farthest I'd ever walked was ten miles as part of a pro-test march back in my California-dreaming days, and that was ten years ago. "I am not from the Pepsi generation, Lord," I reminded Him. "I'm a baby boomer. I can't walk that far."

I decided to try another tactic. I cleared my throat and said forcefully, "I'm talking to the Lord right now, Devil. Please leave me alone." However, God repeated Himself, and after hearing it a second time, I knew it was Him talking to me. I didn't question Him, odd sense of humor though He has. I simply said "okay" and started planning the walk of my life—a whole 110 miles from Brewton to the Alabama State Capital in Montgomery. At the time, I thought 110 miles would be the longest distance I would ever walk, a one-time deal. Boy, was I wrong about that!

To this day, it's still amazing how easy it was to plan the walk. First, my close friend Vanessa Kyles helped draft a letter to Governor Riley describing the experiences and plight of the poor in Alabama. Next, we selected a walk date. It was December, and I still needed a few months to prepare, so I decided on March 23, 2004. By then, I figured the weather would be comfortable—not too hot, not too cold. More importantly, there wouldn't be many snakes slithering about the roadsides. I also needed to find a good pair of walking shoes, but I wasn't in a position to spend a fortune on them, as every penny spent on shoes was one less penny the food bank could spend feeding the hungry. I started searching yard sales, hoping for a bargain, and again God intervened. I was blessed to find a new pair of SAS shoes for only ten dollars. They would have cost $140 in an athletic shoe store! God was making sure I had everything I needed.

The hardest part of planning the trip was finding someone to be my shadow driver. This person would follow me in my Chevy truck and keep an eye out for trouble on the road, like dogs or unsafe passes. He or she would be there at break time, providing me a place to sit down and rest. If the weather was bad, the shadow driver would shelter me. I didn't have the money to pay anyone, so the person had to be a volunteer—someone who really believed in the cause. Many people were willing to help out, but, predictably, had schedules that conflicted with the walk. It took two months of searching to find an eligible candidate, or, should I say candidates. Three wonderful souls stepped up and offered to share the duties of the shadow driver during the long walk.

A few months passed and the big day finally arrived. The local newspaper announced the walk the week before, informing the public that it would start at the courthouse at 7 AM. The paper also formally invited the community to see me off or join in. I was prepared to begin my long journey amid a crowd of forty to fifty people, and I hoped they'd join me for the first few miles to get everything off to an upbeat start. My sister Jane had taken off some vacation time so she could shadow drive me for the first two days.

We arrived at the courthouse at 5:30 AM. No one was there, but it was early yet. I was sure my supporters would start turning up a little later, just before the walk began. The minutes started to quickly tick by, and my departure time crept closer and closer. Still, though, no one had shown up. My nerves started to get the better of me as I waited. Finally, the first car arrived, followed closely by another. And then another. But that was it.

Only four people had come to start the walk with me—my friend Vanessa, Stuart, and my twin nieces, Doris and Samantha. They agreed to go as far as the local high school, three miles down the road. Police Chief David Lovelace also kindly made sure I had a police escort to the city limits. But where was everyone else? The morning remained stubbornly quiet and the courthouse steps stubbornly empty. At the very least I had expected my pastor to show up and bless the walk with a prayer, but no one from my church had arrived.

Defeated, I began the walk, my heart heavy with sorrow. As we approached the high school, Valerie Long, a friend, walked up to me and donated fifty dollars. I was thankful for her generosity—this was, after all, a fundraising trip. Soon after, we arrived at the school. My fellow walkers took their leave, and I found myself on my own. That's when the self-pity began. Didn't anyone else share my dream apart from this small handful of people?

It seems so obvious that when a fellow human being is suffering, something needs to be done about it. Why didn't everyone else feel this way? Even if members of the community weren't in a position to help financially, why weren't they at least walking *en masse* to draw the attention of those with the power to do something about it? I was totally confused, but a year later I started to understand why.

In 2005, I was standing on a street corner listening to the radio in Salisbury, North Carolina. They were playing Michael Bublé's "I Wanna Go Home," and I heard this line, *"I know why you could not come along with me; this was not your dream, but you always believed in me."* I understood then that it was me who had the dream. This walk was my way of trying to help the poor. Some people drop off bags of groceries at food banks, others volunteer for Meals on Wheels, and others write letters to Congress or give a few dollars to a hungry man sitting on a street corner. Walking 110 miles for hunger wasn't everyone's thing. We each have our own way of contributing to a cause.

However, as I ventured off on my first walk, I had yet to have this realization. I felt lonely and pessimistic. But I soon found myself on the receiving end of a morale boost. A reporter from WRKG caught up with my shadow driver and me to ask why, exactly, I was walking for hunger. I hoped the telecast would bring others out to share the walk.

"Why am I walking for hunger?" I began, considering. "I could go ahead and talk about food shortages. Heck, I've been trying to do that in my community, and some people might listen. But walking 110 miles for it? That's going to grab peoples' attention. That's going to force people to take a look at exactly what this walk is about, and maybe then realize just how severe the problem is. It takes doing something drastic to make a drastic change." Walking 110 miles, I explained, was certainly radical, and sometimes it took being radical to draw attention to a problem.

Just the fact that somebody was listening put a little spring in my step. I was able to cover fifteen to twenty miles a day easily. The walk was actually relatively pleasant, except for a few difficulties with dogs I encountered along the way.

On the second day, the truck broke down in the best possible place: in front of a mechanic's shop outside Castleberry. The mechanic was wonderful and worked on the truck right away so we could get back on the road. About two hours later, we started back out, but the weather decided not to cooperate. It began to pour cats and, quite literally, dogs. I watched as farther up the road five dogs bolted out of a yard and began to chase the truck. Seeing the ferocious canines, I ran, terrified, and hid behind a church. I waited there until my sister could turn around and double back for me.

All my shadow drivers were well aware of my fear of dogs and on high alert for any problems. I had been scared of being bitten ever since I had walked that "block from hell" in my childhood, and even the sight of a dog could trigger a flashback. Not surprisingly, then, my greatest fear on this walk was vicious dogs. I felt a bit like Little Red Riding Hood, except my problem wasn't a bad wolf; it was a ferocious canine. There were times when the truck had to be right at my side because some of the dogs along the way were so aggressive.

The road can be a lonely place with only your thoughts to keep you company. And thoughts, left to their own devices, can quickly blow themselves out of proportion. On hyper alert for any sign of Cujo, I eventually became so jittery that even cows seemed like a threat. At one point I was wearing my orange safety jacket when I passed a cow pasture. The cows, curious at any diversion, began walking toward the fence line, following the orange jacket. It was likely they were hoping for some kind of feed or treat, but I was so spooked by their mass descent that I took off running and didn't stop until they were out of sight.

Maudie Mae McKinney, a friend who lived in Montgomery, took over driving duties after my sister's shift ended. When she spied me running from the cows, she drove after me in a panic, unsure what the problem was. Revealing to Maudie that I'd been spooked by a pack of pastured cows sounded ridiculous, even to my own ears, and we had a good laugh about it later.

My third shadow driver was my California-dreaming friend, Linda (Lowe) Smith. Linda flew out from Los Angeles just to help me finish the walk. When I arrived at the Montgomery county line, I called my friend Vanessa to share the good news. I was so excited! Jamie Martin, a photographer from the *Mobile Press Register*, was waiting at the city's outskirts to ask me a few questions and snap some photos.

"How do you feel right now?" Jamie asked. "Are you tired, happy, nervous?" He delivered his questions in a rapid-fire manner that had the air of an interrogation.

But I appreciated the interest. "I feel great," I beamed. "This walk is one of my proudest feats, and I would never have been able to do this without the support of God, my shadow drivers, my friends, and my family. Three months ago, I doubted whether or not I could even do this. I feel proud."

I called my mom and told her, in the immortal words of Jimmy Cagney, *"I made it, Ma. I made it, and I'm on top of the world."* That's exactly how it felt, as if everyone the walk represented was out there with me.

The farther I walked into the city, however, the more my euphoria was replaced with anxiety. Little by little the reality of what I was doing was sinking in, and I was becoming increasingly nervous. By the time I turned down Dexter Avenue and saw the State Capitol shining at the top of the hill, I was terrified! My impending meeting with Governor Riley had turned my stomach inside out. I was afraid I wouldn't be able to find the words to make him see the precarious lives of the people I met daily or make him understand what needed to be done to make those lives better. My heart began to race. *What should I say?* I wondered. *What can I do?* Then I remembered my letter—the well-thought out, articulate letter Vanessa had drafted. That letter contained everything I needed to say. Thank God I had that letter.

My legs started shaking as I climbed the Capitol's steps, and not from fatigue. Somehow, I managed to keep moving forward. I pushed open the heavy double doors and entered a huge, beautiful hallway. Two reporters were already there, waiting to see if Governor Riley would meet with me. I was directed to the office of Jessica Flannery, the governor's scheduling secretary. I presented Jessica with the letter and asked if Governor Riley was available. Jessica read the letter slowly, as if she were carefully considering every word. In reality, she was probably just buying time, casting about for a tactful excuse to turn me away.

In the end, she settled on a close version of the truth. "I'm sorry," Jessica said, not meeting my eye. "The governor is busy today and won't be able to meet with you." She didn't offer me an appointment, but, sensing my disappointment, promised, "I will make sure he gets the letter."

"Thank you," I said gracefully, doing my best to fight back the tears that threatened to spill over. A flood of emotions bombarded me. I was tired from the walk. I was angry with a state government that was too busy to care for the people who elected it. I was hurt that I'd been turned away. I was disheartened that my long journey had fallen short at the last hurdle. Everything hit all at once. But I had to muster some composure to face the reporters' questions. *Take the high road,* I thought as I exited Jessica's office. I repeated it silently, over and over, like a mantra.

The reporters were eagerly waiting, sensing a maelstrom of a story in the making. "How do you feel about the governor's refusal to meet with you?" one of them asked. "Do you think your walk was worth it?" another shouted.

My mind flashed through all the things I wanted to say, and it cast about until it landed on something more appropriate. *Take the high road.* "I'm not mad," I said quietly. "I am disappointed that the governor couldn't accept the letter himself. As far as the walk, I am still proud of our accomplishment." At least I could give the press that much truth. My shadow drivers and I had finished a 110-mile walk in six days. We had delivered our letter and brought statewide attention to the hunger issue. Regardless of what happened with the governor, we had accomplished our goal.

But, I must admit, I felt the tiniest bit of satisfaction when Governor Riley caught a fair amount of heat for not meeting with me. That night, the first thing I heard on FOX news was, "How would you like to walk 110 miles to deliver a letter to the governor about hunger, and he doesn't even meet with you?" The governor's office called the next day and told me they would meet with me anytime. I just had to make an appointment, they explained. I knew they were trying to seem reasonable in the face of the backlash. I told them I would see them next year . . . on my way to Washington, DC.

After the walk, the food bank was busier than ever. We received referrals from all over Brewton, and we continued our efforts to seek out people in need of a helping hand. Our outreach began to grow when a nearby community sought to establish their own Meals on Wheels program. The community leaders partnered with a local church and committed to serving twenty-six elderly people a hot meal each day. Carlisa, Inc. would deliver the food.

Demand for food continued to grow, and soon the food bank was serving seventy-nine hot meals per day. The deliveries were spread out over 100 miles. Sadly, the church's Meals on Wheels program didn't last, but the food bank worked to pick up the slack.

Blessedly, the walk had increased the food bank's donations. While the turnout may have been low at the beginning of my journey, it turned out that people were listening after all. We received food and money from all over Alabama and Florida. A local lawyer took an interest in the food bank. He had faith in what we were trying to accomplish and turned out to be a major force in helping us acquire the funds needed to serve others. Soon the food bank was receiving yearly donations from three local foundations and trusts. Their contributions amounted to nearly $25,000. The food bank's dreams of service were becoming a reality.

"Do you think your walk was worth it?" a reporter had asked. The loneliness, the frustrations, the tired legs and sore feet, the vicious dogs, the closed door at the Capitol. But what were those minor things compared to the many people who heard the message and actively responded? It was heartening to our donors to know that the people their money helped were the needy. The food bank reassured them that nothing would be spent on anything other than assisting those who needed it.

Was the walk worth it?

The worth was in knowing that every mouth fed eased an empty stomach. The worth was in knowing that providing small necessities, like gas or food, eased a little human suffering. The worth was in knowing that a community could band together to overcome injustice. Governors and meetings and scandal are minor inconveniences—small blotches that detract from the larger picture. But the larger picture had been seen.

The walk had been completely worth it.

In God's Hands

There was big news. A Category 4 hurricane was bearing down on us. However, unbeknownst to me, Hurricane Ivan did not pose the greatest danger to my life. In September 2004, just a few days before it was due to hit Alabama, I visited my dad, who was in a nursing home. He seemed upset. He told me that he had dreamed one of his girls was going to be very sick. My first thought was of my sister Molly. Little did I know he was talking about me!

I'd been feeling badly for about a week, after taking a fall while building the frame for a deck that I was adding to the food bank kitchen. I had been walking between the boards when I fell through a hole and scraped my leg on the side of the wood. It really hurt, but it didn't look that bad when it happened, so I just thought it would be sore for a while and then go away. But my leg swelled up, and a few days later I started feeling really ill—so much so that I couldn't find the strength to prepare the house for Ivan, our un-welcomed guest (or should I say "gust?"). I was supposed to nail everything down, but instead I just paid the neighbor to tie down as much as possible. In any case, I knew that if Ivan hit as forcefully as predicted, nothing would save my house except the grace of God.

It was September 16, the night the hurricane was to make landfall, and Ivan had been downgraded to a Category 3 storm. My mom and I stayed at my sister Shirley's house. No more driving around in stormy weather for me! By this point, I was feeling so ill that Ivan seemed like a mild irritation by comparison. I knew that the wind howled and roared for hours because, unlike everyone else, I walked the floor the entire night. When morning came, we were relieved that my sister's home was still intact. The entire city had been blessed, because no one had died.

Still, there was a great deal of destruction and a lot of need. Some areas of the city were devastated—it looked as if we were in a war-ravaged third-world country. I couldn't even recognize areas I was familiar with. My mom said it was the worst destruction she had seen in her eighty-three years. And while the powers that be were slow and dragged their feet in sending help to Brewton, our mayor, Ted Jennings, made sure our little town got the aid we needed.

The whole city was without power and the phone lines were down, so I stayed with my mom until things got back to normal. Besides, I was still feeling terribly ill. My family was worried about me, so I promised my sister Jane that if I didn't feel better in a few days, I would go to the hospital. I went home to check on things two days after the storm. It was a Saturday. I felt blessed to find that only half of the roof of my house was gone and only the deck of the food bank was destroyed—-the same deck I'd been building when I took that fall. Fortunately, no trees were down in my yard. Everything in the freezers, however, had started to thaw.

While I was there, Melanie from the utility company came by and of-fered me a job feeding out-of-state workers who were coming to town to help with the cleanup operation. I would feed about 300 workers three meals a day, seven days a week. She told me money was no object. I accepted the job and told her I'd see them on Monday. I asked my sister Jane if she would lend a hand, and I lined up two more people to help. The money from this job would help many more people in the future, but I knew I'd have to do something about my health if I was going to manage the work. So I asked my sister to accompany me to the emergency room in Conecuh County, where she worked. I figured they'd give me a shot and send me on my way. Boy, was I wrong. They admitted me!

My sister and I hoped it would be just an overnight stay, so I would be able to get going with preparations for the job I'd been offered. But as I lay there putting the events of the last few days together in my mind, it suddenly hit me. I called Jane.

"I get it," I said. "I understand what's going on."

"What's going on with what?" she asked. I could hear the confusion in her voice.

"That job with the utility company isn't going to happen."

"What do you mean? Why won't it happen?"

"It's not real. We were duped."

"I have no idea what you are talking about." Jane now sounded exasperated. "What kind of meds do they have you on?"

"I'm thinking perfectly clear. The job wasn't real. God knew I wouldn't go to the doctor for myself. He knew I wouldn't go for anyone else, either. I would go, however, to get that money in order to help people."

Jane still seemed a bit confused.

"God knew that was the only way I'd get medical attention," I continued. "You'll see. That job will not materialize."

"You think so?" Jane asked.

"Yes," I said. "We're not going to see a penny of that money." And we didn't.

So there I was, lying in bed, while everyone else was cleaning up the mess from Ivan. I stayed in the hospital for four days. When I made it back home, I found a note on my door that the food bank wanted me to help pass out food. Unfortunately, I couldn't do it. I was just too weak to participate in the recovery, which broke my heart. Just when my community needed me the most, I couldn't be there for them.

A couple of weeks later, we found out the real reason why the utility company had offered me the job. I was referred to a specialist in Florida, who told me the infection I had was so bad that I would have died if I had gone another couple of days without treatment. God had sent Melanie with the job offer, and I had immediately gone to the doctor. My sister and I had been planning to go to the hospital on Monday, two days after Melanie's visit. It would have been a terrible mistake to wait. God took care of me. He arranged everything so that I would get the help I needed.

I recovered in time to help with the tail-end of the cleanup process. I also had to sort out the mess at my home, with the help of a handyman. The power had been out for so long that Carlisa, Inc. had lost all its frozen food. I would have to wait for more donations before I could replenish the food bank. But I was one of the fortunate ones. It took a while for Brewton to get going again, but everyone pulled together, helped each other, and got it done. The truth was that I wasn't really needed; after large-scale disasters, people come out of the woodwork to do their bit. God had it all under control. After realizing that, I felt refreshed, peaceful, close to God, grateful, cleansed, and renewed. Most of all, I felt blessed to be alive and thankful that I would be able to continue to help others when I was well enough again.

Hundreds of volunteers from all over the country gave their time to get us back on track. There are no words to express how wonderful people are in times of crisis. If only they would realize that a permanent crisis is taking place every day and that struggling, hungry people need their help. What a fine world it would be!

That was, of course, part of the message I wanted to get out with my planned walk from Brewton to Washington, DC. Oh, yes. When I'd told the folks at Governor Riley's office I'd stop over on my way to DC, it wasn't just idle talk! I was indeed going to walk 928 miles from Brewton to the White House to deliver a letter to the President. During the lonely six-day walk to Montgomery, I'd had several long conversations with God. He had, in His ineffable way, communicated to me that I would carry the same letter about hunger in the nation to President Bush.

But as I lay idle recovering from my illness, I kept wondering if I'd be able to make it. I prayed for a full recovery in time for the start date, March 22, 2005. I thought of my illness as God's way of testing my faith and my commitment to end hunger. Concerned friends kept saying that I could use my ill health as an excuse not to walk, but I knew I would hit the road. There would be no excuses. It was God's will, and He would take care of me. As Joel Osteen wrote on one of his blogs:

> Sometimes God asks us to do things that don't make sense. It doesn't seem logical. It doesn't fit into our budget. It doesn't line up with our schedule. "God, You want me to go back to college? I'm forty years old." "God, You want me to give them a gift? I was saving those funds for my own dreams." "God, You want me to leave this secure position that I've had for years and start my own business?" Too often we overanalyze it. We debate it. We look at it only in the natural. We end up making excuses, talking ourselves out of it. "That couldn't be God." But if you're going to reach your highest potential, you have to have bold obedience. That means you just do it even when it doesn't make sense. That's what faith is all about.[1]

---

1   Joel Osteen, "Discover the Champion in You," sermon delivered at Lakewood Church in Houston, Texas, on Sunday, October 13, 2013.

I soon got back into doing my hot food route, which at that stage involved delivering seventy-three meals a day. The first day out, I found one of my elderly charges, poor Ms. Phelps, on the floor in her house. She had fallen the day before and had been on the floor all night long. I tried to help her up, but she was too heavy. I ended up calling the police. I thought about how long she could have stayed on the floor if I hadn't shown up. It made me realize how important it was for someone to touch base with people like her every day. We started delivering to some of our food recipients seven days a week.

All too soon, the time drew near for the walk to Washington, DC. I had to start making preparations for my elderly folks. We provided some of them with grocery store gift cards so they wouldn't run out of food before I returned. The extremely vulnerable ones, such as Ms. Phelps, needed someone to check in on them every day. It took some effort to get everything situated. I left money and found someone to deliver hot meals while I was gone. A friend, Augustus Rankins (1952–2014), agreed to babysit the food bank by answering the phone and distributing food.

Our local newspaper, *The Brewton Standard,* called to discuss the walk shortly before I was to leave. They offered me a mobile phone, but I already had one. I also had my new SAS shoes, and I'd had three signs painted on the van. The first read, "We all know who won the 2004 *American Idol,* but do we know if our neighbors are hungry?" The second read, "We are walking to end hunger in America." The third read, "We are walking to end hunger and abolish the death penalty in America."

Since my first walk to Montgomery in 2004, I'd joined an organization named Alabama Arise, a non-profit citizens' policy and advocacy group. One of their priorities for 2005 was to reform the death penalty laws in Alabama, a matter that was, and is, close to my heart. Apart from the cruelty involved (especially when an execution is botched), my main concern was that it was all too probable that innocent people were being executed in the name of justice. The ability to pay, the color of the perpetrator, and the color of the victim seemed to unfairly determine who ended up on death row.

The poor were at the greatest disadvantage. Alabama had no public defender's office and paid the least of any state to court-appointed attorneys. Often, these attorneys had no experience in criminal law. Almost one in four inmates on death row was there because the judge, with an eye toward re-election, had overridden the jury's recommendation. To make matters worse, the courts had denied post-conviction DNA testing in some cases, which meant that the person—usually a poor person—had been sentenced to death based on circumstantial evidence. If one takes into account the possibility of false or fallible witnesses, the risk of corrupt or negligent cops on any given case, biased juries, and political maneuverings, the chances were quite high that a few innocent people were ending up on death row.

Therefore, if for no other reason, I felt that the death penalty laws had to be reformed to eliminate the chance of taking an innocent person's life. I can't even imagine someone sitting on death row waiting to be executed for a crime he or she didn't commit. It was heartbreaking. These were people's sons, daughters, brothers, sisters, and fathers. These were my people. Their need was so great, and there was so little I could do for them. A hungry person could be fed, but what could I do for the person who was about to be murdered by the state? All I could do was raise my voice on their behalf and hope that enough people—the *right* people—would listen. In short, though my primary focus remained feeding those imprisoned by hunger, I was now also calling for the poor to stop being put to death in the name of justice.

So, with the big day approaching, I became increasingly excited, but also more and more nervous. It was a much longer distance than the last walk, which would mean more vicious dogs, more snakes, and longer hours of loneliness. Would my legs hold up? And what about old Frank, a customer from the restaurant who had offered to shadow drive me the whole way? He was old, absentminded, and prone to falling asleep at the drop of a hat. Would he be able to cope? And how would I be received as I passed through each state?

I kept reassuring myself that everything would be all right. God would have my back. The walk was His will and this was His mission—to bring to the country's attention that Hurricane Hunger was gusting through America each day and to call on my fellow Americans to share in the infectious joy of doing something about it.

PART II

～

Journal Entries for the Walk of Life

CHAPTER ONE

Extraordinary Encounters in Everyday Experiences

God, help me. Am I out of my mind? It's 7:21 AM and forty-eight de-grees. I'm going on two hours of sleep. I don't want to get out of bed. It's warm in here and freezing out there.

What are you complaining about, Lisa? There are innocent people on death row being punished for crimes they didn't commit. They can't make the choice whether to stay in bed or leave their house. You can.

But there's nothing like sleeping in your own bed. Do I really have to say goodbye to it? Fifty days to not be in my cozy bed is a long time. I don't have to do this. No one is forcing me into it. In fact, everyone around me is begging me NOT to go!

There's a thin layer of frost on my bedroom window. I can see my breath. Nature's "good morning" sure doesn't seem all that friendly today. But I have a choice . . .

I start the kettle. Step into the shower *(come on, pipes, give me some hot water . . . I won't have another hot shower for who knows how long . . .)*

Coffee. Eggs. Sneakers. The soles are brand new.

Wait . . . what am I thinking? I'm not an athlete. I'm not young. I'm a middle-aged woman. Is devotion to my mission enough to get me through this?

I *could* just crawl back into bed. Maybe I feel a cold coming on? *Cough . . . cough . . .* My family and friends would be relieved if I just stayed home and forgot about all this silliness. But I made a commitment, didn't I?

Sure, other folks are getting out of bed to a cold morning, too. The difference? They're clocking in for a 9 to 5. I'm clocking in for 900 miles! I'll trudge along highways, through unknown neighborhoods, cross paths with vicious dogs, and venture—finally—into the political wilderness of Washington, DC.

My goal? To deliver a letter to President George Bush, addressing the state of the poor in Alabama and asking to abolish the death penalty. But first I have to get ready—yes, there's still that. I break down my morning preparations, just as I planned the fifty-day trek ahead.

Coffee. Eggs . . . Where was I? Oh, yeah, the brand-new sneakers . . .

Oh, my word. These sneakers make noise when I walk. Are they going to squeak from here all the way to the Capitol building? At least the traffic will hear me before they see me. Maybe I won't be road kill after all.

Can I do this?

Yes, I can. Why? Because I'm not alone. God, through His love and wisdom, shone a light on this path before me—all 900 gorgeous miles. I have an opportunity to see this mission through, with His help. All I have to do is follow Him, follow His path, no matter what I encounter along the way. No matter what creature pursues me—whether the four-legged or two-legged kind—God always has my back.

Now it's time for me to have God's back. Why must innocent people be put to death for crimes they didn't commit? Man doesn't have the right to decide who lives and dies. Only God has that right.

As sure as the sun shines every morning, bringing warmth and life—and the sun *will* shine this morning, eventually—God gives us opportunities to walk out in faith. This morning is another opportunity. God has already provided many blessings. Many kind souls volunteered shelter, food, or a hug of encouragement for the trek ahead.

God also brought me a shadow driver—Frank Mason. He's an unusual guardian angel. Sure, Frank is ready to turn in his van for a Rascal scooter (he's seventy-one), and he swerves when he sees a woman (luckily, that happens only fifty-one percent of the time), but to have another pair of eyes and ears to spot dangers during my travels is absolutely priceless.

And there *will* be dangers. However, the obstacles I encounter will add some much needed contrast. Obstacles highlight my life's limitless rewards. I'm astonished as I wonder what gestures of human kindness, humor, and generosity will surely await me on the path ahead.

Why keep a journal? Because there's no better time to indulge in some heavy introspective thinking than when you have nothing to do except put one foot in front of the other. This daily journal will serve to remind me of my journey—the ups, the downs, and, hopefully, the not-too-many sideways. There are a lot of roads on which to get lost between Brewton, Alabama, and Washington, DC!

Speaking of putting one foot in front of the other . . . *is it 7:34 AM already?* Time to start with the first step—the first of many. Will you join me?

CHAPTER TWO

Alabama

MARCH 22, 2005–APRIL 2, 2005

March 22: Brewton, Alabama

There were quite a few deliveries I had to make before starting the journey. (Who am I kidding? The journey had already begun.)

Three students from Montgomery had heard about my walk and offered to take time off during spring break to help me with my last-minute deliveries. We had groceries to bring to several elderly people in the neighborhood. I'd be saying goodbye to a dozen more people before I stepped out of Brewton today.

My walk would officially begin outside my front door. During my last walk I had expected too much from other people, so this time I was prepared to take it for what it was. But I got a surprise when I arrived back home. Lydia Grimes, a fan/reporter from *The Brewton Standard*, was waiting for me. She wanted to cover the event. Yes, she actually called it an "event!" It felt good that the cause was finally being taken seriously.

The walk from my home to the highway was hardly a parade. No floats. No confetti. Just me, three students, a small group of friends, and Frank shadowing us in the van. Just before starting this biggest adventure of my life, my legs turned to spaghetti. I was trembling all over. My hands were sweaty. My throat felt tight, and I thought I couldn't breathe. I was terrified.

No one saw my last-minute jitters, but I mentioned them to my friend Ruby. "Why am I doing this?" I said in a terrified voice. "What's wrong with me?"

"Don't go," she said.

For a second I considered the idea, but then my nervousness faded away.

A few others had promised to start the walk with me, but when the time came they made all sorts of excuses as to why they couldn't come. I understood. Really, I did. People get busy. It all comes down to priorities.

I had to make a decision, right then and there—what was my priority? Was it the status quo? Or was my priority to make a change and help spread God's message? I could help people understand the plight of the poor. I could spread the word about how the innocent are being judged by man and sent to die. *I could do this.*

We all have our ways of spreading God's love, and God was giving me my opportunity right at that moment. I could feel the sun warm the top of my head. The heat traveled down my spine, through my legs, and into my shoes. It filled my shoes like buckets of gold until I was steady on my feet.

I imagined the sunlight was God embracing me. Supporting me. I found that I didn't have spaghetti legs anymore. I clasped Ruby's hand and told her everything was going to be okay.

From there, the three students walked with me for about a mile as we headed toward Castleberry. An anti-death penalty activist I knew joined us on the first five miles up North Highway 31. I thought it was fitting that she met us at the start, because she was the one who had taught me about the death penalty and what it meant to be on death row in Alabama. After learning the facts about the justice system, I had decided that I would be happy to walk in support of changing some of the laws in Alabama.

I parted ways with my walking companions, and soon I could hear nothing but the wheels of Frank behind me. The morning sun vanished behind gray clouds. I hoped it wouldn't rain, but just to throw a wrench in my plan, the "weather gods" decided to direct a severe thunderstorm my way. I was forced to sit it out for a few hours until it cleared up. During that time, I had the opportunity to think about the task that was ahead for Frank and me. I decided that no matter what happened, we were going to complete our task, deliver the letters, and change the fate of the poor in this country.

Once the weather improved, I got back up on my feet. *The people have cleared out,* I thought, *and the weather has cleared up. I'm on my own, except for Frank.* He had parked too far ahead of me, and I felt lonely. It was only the first day and already I had to remind myself why I was doing this.

I quickened my step and, despite the bad weather, made it well past

Castleberry. Frank and I decided to travel back to my home for the first two nights. We knew we had at least fifty days of roughing it ahead, and we figured it would be our last two days of comfort. Well, sort of—we had fixed up the van to make it super cozy. We had long pillow beds lining the walls and had the seats fully reclined. Still, thank goodness, I was able to come back to sleep at my place for the night.

When I arrived, I found that the students had left the back door to the house wide open. Hah! Did I have to do everything myself?

"Better is a little with the fear of the Lord, than great treasures and turmoil with it" (Proverbs 15:16).

March 23: Evergreen, Alabama

What's the plan today? Walking from Castleberry to Evergreen. It was a little more than twenty miles. If I could average twenty miles a day, I'd be doing all right.

The name made me smile. *Evergreen.* It reminded me of something that was always green and full of life, which was how I felt walking with God. Despite my sore legs and feet, walking to Evergreen eased the pain. Evergreen offered the promise that abundant generosity would overflow throughout the day.

Of course, this generous "overflowing abundance" included breakfast. Why did the cooks at the drive-thru that morning have to be so generous with the hash browns? After Frank and I wolfed down our meal, I felt a greasy anchor in my stomach. And when Frank dropped me off where we stopped the day before, I wondered if twenty miles would get me back to feeling normal again. Maybe I'd have to walk forty miles to work off this grease-ball of a breakfast.

This gastrointestinal malaise passed as soon as Sandra Preyer, my cousin, showed her sunny face. It thought it was awfully sweet of her to track me down early on my walk to say hi. On top of that, she unexpectedly donated five dollars to the cause. I was touched. If I had any lingering doubts about the walk, they disappeared when Sandra came along. Why? Because Sandra didn't have a lot of money, yet here she was, wanting to donate the little she had. It came straight from her heart.

I thought about the woman in the Bible who put everything she had into the temple collection. *"For they gave a tiny part of their surplus, but she, poor as she is, has given everything she had to live on*" (Mark 12:44). Sandra's donation set the tone for the day.

I continued along the road less traveled—on foot, anyway—until I heard some men hollering, "Hey!" I ignored them and kept walking. I needed to maintain my focus on the long (very long) road ahead.

"Hey, lady!" a voice said again. I turned my head to see a group of highway workers. One of the guys was looking directly at me.

"Hey, lady! Where you walking to?"

It didn't sound so rude in person. After all, he had the highway traffic to compete with. He had probably hollered so loud because he saw my look of determination. Someone with 860 miles to walk ahead of them tends to have that kind of look. It was early in the game, and already each step required concerted effort.

"You lost, lady?" he asked.

I pointed to the van—the one Frank was driving right behind me. "See that van?" I said. "That's what I'm doing." I stopped so Frank would stop, giving the highway worker a moment to read the signs. I watched him closely. Still, I wasn't sure how he was going to react.

It usually took people a few minutes to read everything. I had started playing a game with myself. As I watched people's facial expressions as they read, I asked myself, *Is this a pro-capital-punishment type person or an only-God-can-take-a-life type?* So far, I had come across quite a few of the pro-capital-punishment types.

The highway worker with the extremely vocal vocal cords crossed the street. He dodged oncoming traffic. It reminded me of that videogame Frogger, except this guy was really good at it. I guess it comes with the territory of the job.

I stayed put, still unsure whether he was going to shake my hand or start an argument. He rolled up his sleeves.

Oh no, I thought. *This is just like the movies.* I imagined we were in the Wild West and it was a showdown. I was on one side of the street and this man on the other.

He came closer and took off his orange vest. "You're going to need this more than I do," he said cheerfully. Well, that was unexpected.

"Thank you so much!" I said. "May God bless you!" And there it was … that moment of pure joy washing over me. *Oh, my God, this is what You made us for—to give and receive, to love and be loved.* My heart was spilling with gratitude. I gave the generous soul a big bear hug.

I put on my new orange vest. Funny, orange wasn't usually my best color, but today it suited me. Although I was already deeply committed to my walk, putting on the vest "initiated" me in a way. I could walk with even greater confidence than before. The uniform felt official.

Frank and I made it to Evergreen. Of course, Frank was ready to stretch his legs after driving behind me for so long. I had the opposite feeling. All I wanted was to get off my feet and sit down.

While we were taking a much-deserved rest, a hippie approached. He was white, over forty, and had a long ponytail. He offered his hand and asked who we were. I guess he could tell by the van that we were *something*.

"My name's Lisa," I said, and then pointed next to me. "That's Frank. He's my shadow driver. I run a small non-profit food bank kitchen back in Brewton called Carlisa, Inc. I'm walking to Washington, DC!"

"From Brewton?" The man couldn't believe it.

"Yeah, but I'm stopping in Montgomery first to have a chat with Governor Riley about the state of hunger that is currently plaguing us. I'm hoping I can talk to President Bush, too, when I get to DC. I want to discuss the poverty situation that is occurring across our nation and see what we can do to make a change."

"Mind if I walk a few miles with you?" he asked.

"Does a brown bear eat people?" I replied.

The hippie had a name—Larry. Larry and I walked and talked. He was on the road himself, playing his guitar for nursing home residents.

"That's incredible!" I said. "The residents at our nursing home in Brewton would love to hear you play."

"Really?" he said. "You think there's a place I could park my van for the night?"

"There is." I hesitated for a moment. "But how about you just come back with Frank and me to my place? We're going to spend the night there and then come back in the morning to pick up where we left off."

Larry and I walked another three miles before he decided to turn around and head to Brewton. I gave him directions to get to the nursing home, and then directions to get from the nursing home to my place. I finished my twenty miles for the day and headed back home with Frank. Larry was waiting for us in the front yard when we pulled up.

"Come on inside," I said. "You can use the shower to clean up, and I'll wash your clothes. Maybe I'll even make you some dinner."

I was surprised at how much energy I had. Even though I had been on my feet all day, walking alongside trucks and trees and trash, it felt good to prepare a hot meal for Larry. Isn't that what God intended?

Today was a blessed day. So much generosity. My cousin Sandra donating the little she had. The highway worker giving me his orange vest. Larry's company toward the end of the day. It truly fulfilled me. I was blessed. I realized generosity is a nutrient that we all need to survive. And when we receive this goodwill, we want nothing more than to give it back in kind.

I prepared a hot meal. Frank, Larry, and I sat around and ate. There was a lot of talking and laughing, and then some "yaying" and "naying" afterward when we watched *American Idol.* Larry and I talked late into the night. Good food, good company, good times.

Tomorrow would be another day. I may not come across a Sandra or Larry to keep me company when I got lonely out there, but I was thankful to God for giving me these moments to cherish and remember.

Oh, my God, You saw my loneliness and filled my heart to capacity. Thank You, thank You. And thank You for giving me the chance to do the same for others and advertise the need.

March 24: McKenzie, Alabama

As I mentioned, Frank and I had decided that since we were going to rough it for nearly two months, we might as well enjoy the proximity to home as long as we could. For the past two nights we had driven back to my place. I had slept in my bed. Cooked in my kitchen. But this morning would be the last time.

Come on, Lisa. Get up and see what Frank and Larry are doing.

Larry was in the yard, preparing to leave. I gave him some canned goods, forty dollars, and a farewell embrace. We said our goodbyes, and then Frank and I took off toward McKenzie. The weather was beautiful, and I was thankful for having been introduced to a new friend. But something started nagging at me. My feet were already getting sore. Sure, I had anticipated some pain, but not this early in the walk.

I had walked more than forty-five miles in the last three days. I couldn't remember the last time I had walked that much, but my feet did—*never.* The pain was mild but great enough to make its presence known.

I hear you, feet. You're tired and sore. But don't give up yet, dear feet.

Something God taught me over the years was that when I was feeling pain, sometimes the best thing to do to relieve it was share in the pain of others. I had the opportunity when an elderly man stopped to chat just outside of Evergreen. He had a lot to say about hunger. Many of his elderly neighbors were living on next to nothing. I told him of the dozens of hungry in Brewton. He was grateful that I was speaking up for his friends who were going without.

I promised I would do my best to bring visibility to the hungry in America. Suddenly, my sore-feet problems didn't seem like real problems anymore.

The elderly man showed me his garden, which included an enormous berry bush. The dewberries sparkled in the sunlight like giant purple tears. The effect was astonishing. I was reminded of the burning bush on Mount Sinai—about Moses receiving the Word. Tears filled my eyes. I realized the road so far hadn't been that tough, and I was comforted in knowing how blessed I was to have a voice and God's love behind me. I had the will to bring attention to the hunger issue in America—to give a voice to those who didn't always have the chance to speak up for themselves.

The kind man invited me to help myself. I gathered the glistening berries, eating a berry here and there, until my palms were red with juice. The sweet fruits surprised my tongue.

A hen walked over and started pecking underneath the bush. She enjoyed tasting the berries too, and she was quick to pick up one when it rolled out of my hand and fell to the ground. I decided to drop a few more on purpose. I could have dropped berries all the way to Washington, DC, and she would have followed behind picking them up!

Further into McKenzie, a man stopped to warn us of the strange people in that neck of the woods. He seemed a bit shifty, and I wondered if the "strange people" he referred to might be himself. I watched him read the sign on the van about the death penalty. I didn't have to guess whether he was a pro-capital-punishment type person.

"You don't believe in an eye for an eye?" he croaked.

"Not in this case," I said. "I believe in 'vengeance is mine, sayeth the Lord.'" The man excused himself, and our friendly conversation ended there.

Farther on, two college students related to one of our supporters joined me for about an hour. I could not thank them enough for their company.

Frank picked me up after I had walked twenty miles, and we drove back to a truck stop in Evergreen. It was strange to be driving those twenty miles instead of walking them. When you're walking all that way, mostly alone with only your thoughts to keep you company, you cover much more mental ground than just twenty ol' miles.

I peered out the windows and looked into the woods to try to see the "strange people" the man in McKenzie had mentioned. When we reached the truck stop, we decided not to take any chances. Frank reclined on a seat, and I slept on a mat on the floor. It reminded me of the first time I'd spent the night in a van. It had been the '80s, and my family and I were visiting a relative in Delaware. We were short of beds, so my nephews and I spent the night in my sister Shirley's van. This was same van that we had turned into a rolling store some years later.

It rained all night, and Frank and I slept like logs at that truck stop. To this day, when rain is predicted, I go outside, make up a bed in the van, and sleep like a baby.

Oh, dear God, bless all Your children as You have blessed us this night.

March 25: Georgiana, Alabama

Frank and I didn't encounter any "strange people" during the night. We had a sound, restful sleep. There was really only one thing so far on my journey that had sent shivers down my spine. And it wasn't people. . .

Big, small, loud, quiet, hairy, or fluffy . . . *that's* what had been giving me the heebie-jeebies. No, scratch that. *That's* what had downright *scared* me the last four days. The D-O-G-S. Sure, to the owners, these dogs were "Snickers," "Little Bit," or "Lassie." But to me they were ferocious mouths with shark-like teeth on legs.

Because there were not dog ordinances in these parts, the canines ran loose—and often ran loose right toward me! Fortunately, today I had company. Not only was the weather beautiful, but also Carlisa and her sister, Kondra, accompanied me to Georgiana. Another friend, Bill Williams, joined me as well. A musician, Bill was also a strong supporter of abolishing the death penalty. After hearing about my walk from a mutual friend, anti-death-penalty-activist Bill drove all the way down from Birmingham to walk with me.

Bill parked his car a little bit farther down the road and joined me to walk fourteen miles to Greenville. It had been by far the best walking day for me. My feet didn't complain too much. I was in the company of good friends.

And Bill was a fast walker. Plus, he wasn't afraid of dogs.

Today, when a big black German shepherd—uninvited—joined us on the road, we walked by without looking twice. Ah, to be on the road for a full day without worrying about ferocious beasts. What a feeling! I wished I could always be that brave.

Uh, oh . . . I spoke too soon about my feet . . .

In retrospect, it wasn't all that bad. Because my feet were acting up, they prompted me to stop and visit a tiny mom-n-pop store, which ended up being a magical experience. We were all were ready for a break—not just my poor old feet. We bought some hoop cheese and crackers and washed it down with a nice cold Coke. It reminded me of my cotton field days, sitting under a shady tree waiting for a cool breeze to come along. The owners were friendly and allowed us to sit there for as long as we liked. We stayed and watched the people coming and going. Black people came in and enjoyed the company of the white storeowners, and vice versa. Seeing this filled my heart with hope—and that hope would keep me going, sore feet and all!

"Are you wearing a bulletproof vest?" said a voice.

Huh? I almost choked on a mouthful of cheese. Gee, that came out of nowhere. I glanced toward the direction of the voice. The comment settled in. I went from surprised to shocked . . . and then scared.

A black man approached the table. Was this guy serious? Yes, he was. And he was waiting for my response.

"No," I said, "I'm not wearing a bulletproof vest. Why?"

The man cracked a smile. "You're walking down the highway with a sign on a vehicle talking about the death penalty with a white man. Do I need to say any more?"

Thank goodness Bill was in the men's room. He might have been offended. Frank thought it was the funniest thing he'd ever heard. He couldn't stop laughing.

That night, after finishing our walk and taking Bill back to his car, we spent the night at a twenty-four-hour gas station. As I drifted off to sleep, I couldn't help but think about what the man had said in the store. In a way, I guess he was right. Maybe I should have been more concerned for my safety. But I just wasn't.

As I rested, I tried to figure out the logic behind my fears. Here I was terrified of dogs, but not scared about what might happen to me walking 900 miles with a controversial sign on my car.

Now, if they could come up with a dog-proof vest . . . that'd I'd buy in a second.

Oh, Lord, save Your people . . . save our people . . . and bless Your inheritance.

March 26: Natural Dangers

Day five. Forty-five more days to go. Yikes. Is that right? Forty-five more days? I recounted. Yes, that's right.

Yesterday was a fine day of walking with friends and spreading God's Word. Yesterday, not only were people generous with their time, but also the sun was generous with its rays. Today wasn't the same. Today was a different day.

I was all alone. Except for Frank, of course, who now shadow-drove in front of me. It sure got lonely walking far behind the shadow of the van. We had decided the last couple of days it would be safer for Frank to drive ahead. That way, he would be able to see in the rearview mirror what kind of trouble was coming my way.

Today, trouble came in the form of thunder. And hail. And lightning. "Nature's wrath" type stuff, you know? The weather was rotten, which reflected the solitude I was feeling. There was even a hailstorm. But no storm could compare to the one I brewed up with Frank when he almost *got me killed.* Not on purpose. At least, I don't think so.

Did he regret taking on the job as my shadow driver? Was he purposefully sabotaging the walk so we could go back home and forget this whole thing? There was no time to ask these questions when the thunder pounded the sky and the lightning snapped. There was just time to *get in the van!* And QUICK!

Where was Frank? I shielded my eyes from the icy rocks falling from the sky. I couldn't find the van. He wasn't just up ahead as we had planned. When the lightning picked up, it seemed to strike the ground all around me. I ran like heck. My shoes were soaking wet, and I managed to step in every puddle on my sprint up the road. Finally, I caught a glimpse of the van around a curve.

I imagined how cozy Frank was inside. The heater was on, surely. Perhaps the radio. He was probably nibbling on something, too. And here I was, so uncomfortable, and . . . well, in danger!

As I ran, my eyes darted around, hoping to find other objects the lightning might strike. A tree? Yes. A flagpole? Yes. A telephone pole? Yes. Plenty of objects much taller than my five-foot-eight-inch height. Surely the lightning would aim for one of those fine inanimate objects.

KABOOOOOOOM! Yikes! The lightning flashes seemed to lick my heels.

I screamed at Frank when I reached the van. "Are you nuts, or what? Don't you know what a shadow driver is? Or do you just not care? You got to be more careful!" I might have added a few choice expletives as I nearly pulled the passenger door off the hinges. But, I mean, really! I was scared outta my wits.

Frank was surprised to see me. And what did he do? "Close the door, Lisa. You're letting the heat out."

I curled my fist in frustration. Oh, my goodness, I had entrusted my safety to someone who was two cards short of a full deck!

He laughed. The nerve! "A little lightning ain't gonna hurt nobody."

It was lunchtime. Actually, it was well before lunchtime, but shoot—I needed a break from the storm. At Frank's request, we stopped at a small café for some lunch. He hoped it would improve my mood.

I, on the other hand, was rattled. Sometimes when you're in a life-or-death situation, your instincts kick in. Maybe because the fight-or-flight part of you takes over and you don't have time to fret over your emotions. The emotions and the fretting come over you afterward. Like a tsunami.

Yeah, I had the jitters. I couldn't eat. The food was cold. I'm not even sure it was real food. I felt bad for not eating the offerings, as the restaurant owners were sweet. They gave us complimentary bottled water for our trip. I still felt rotten. What do I do when I feel rotten? Take it out on a creature one-millionth my size. Reasonable, right?

When I got back on the road, I started destroying large ant mounds. There were hundreds of them lining the sides of the highway, so I was pretty busy for at least a few hours. I made a game of it. I pretended I was a hit woman who'd been hired to destroy all the anthills because some worker ants were planning a hostile takeover of the presidential palace ant mound in Utah.

Each time I destroyed a mound, I'd say, "You thought you were going to take over the presidential palace?" Then I'd stand back and watch the ants spread out before I continued down the road. Of course, I could be next. I came across a long black snake, probably four feet long, directly in my path. I felt my fight-or-flight reflexes kick in. I had to come up with a plan of action. The closer I got to the snake, though, the clearer it became that this poor fellow was dead. Nevertheless, it put me on high alert. The grass on each side of the road was high, so I needed to be careful.

Oh, Lord, save me from snakes and mean spirits.

I felt terribly vulnerable. The road to joy is paved with pitfalls and dangers. This day was one of those that reminded me in whom I should really be putting my trust and how fallible I was. I needn't get too high and mighty about my grand mission.

Oh, Lord, save me from myself.

March 27: Montgomery, Alabama

He's watching me. His beady little eyes can see me a mile away. Maybe if I . . .

That's how much of the day began. Me, trying to outsmart "man's best friend." Of course, the furry rascals were someone else's best friend—not mine. As I walked down a residential street, I zigzagged from one sidewalk to the other. I thought this would be the best way to avoid attracting the attention of the nearby dogs. I could hear them barking, even in my sleep! These dogs were inside my head.

One was even sitting out in the front yard, as if expecting me. The mutt! So I headed to the other side of the street. Unfortunately, the dog I was trying to avoid ran after me. "Bark! Bark! Bark!"

Yep, he did the usual, bark-snarl-bark salute. I was sure this time that I would be attacked. As I was imagining how many stitches I would get if I were lucky enough to be taken to the hospital in time, a car drove by. Phew! That scared him off!

I realized that my fear of dogs was going to become an even bigger problem. In this region, there were dogs everywhere. I stopped for a moment and asked God to take away my fear of dogs. I knew I had to have faith, but I didn't want Him to test it by sending a big Rottweiler my way. I could just see myself two steps ahead of the dog, running down the street, screaming like a banshee!

As the weather worsened, the dogs opted for the comfort of their homes over harassing me. My mind went to other matters. Important ones. Like what was I going to say when I sat down with Governor Riley? I needed to come up with a game plan—a way of speaking that would provide the most effective impact to discuss the plight of the poor in Alabama and the unfairness of the death penalty.

The impending meeting gave me much to think and strategize over. Still, even with such huge matters at stake, I couldn't help but dwell on the mundane. One hundred and ten miles was a huge distance, especially to cover in five days of walking. I looked down and thought, *I should've shed a few pounds by now.*

Before setting out, I'd considered how cumbersome it was going to be to lug the extra pounds everywhere I went, so I was looking forward to losing a few on the walk. Perhaps that's why there were so many dogs in my path. They certainly put a little pep in my step. The extra exercise could help me reach my goal. It just proved that something positive could come out of the worst circumstance.

Lord, forgive me for not having enough faith.

Do I hate dogs? Of course not! In fact, on quite a few occasions I have come to their rescue.

Oh, Lord, bless all our furry friends. And bless our meeting with the governor tomorrow.

Frank and I split the cost to spend the night at a cheap hotel. We wanted to clean up for our meeting with the governor. Besides, it was our last chance to spoil ourselves before we started the long walk to Washington.

March 28: Meeting with Governor Bob Riley

Frank and I got up early, got cleaned up, and started our final leg into downtown Montgomery. I walked down residential streets and did the street shuffle to avoid dogs. After about two hours, I turned down Dexter Avenue and stood for a minute in awe. There it was again—a sight for sore eyes.

My eyes began to water. I was so excited to see it. Yet the closer I got to the Capitol, the farther the building seemed to move away. Our meeting was at 10:00, and I made it with just fifteen minutes to spare. When I arrived at the State Capitol, I felt *déjà vu* walking up those long steps. A couple of reporters asked me questions even before I opened the two huge doors to meet with Governor Riley.

"How is the walk going?"

"How do you feel about your meeting with the governor?"

"Do you have any regrets about the walk? Would you do it again?"

My responses were short and to the point. I was focused on my meeting and didn't want anything to distract me.

"The walk is going great."

"I feel good about my meeting with the governor. I hope it will result in something positive for the people of Alabama."

"No regrets. I just wish the dogs would give me a break. Yes, I would do it again and with pleasure."

The anti-death penalty activist who had joined me for the first five miles of the walk met me at the Capitol building to help me speak with the governor about Alabama's death penalty issues. We went inside, and I greeted the governor with a hug. "I'm sorry for the flack you received for not meeting with me last year," I said. It was partially true.

"That's okay," he said, though I'm sure he was actually less than pleased. He invited me into his office, where we discussed the plight of the poor in Alabama.

"We have elderly people who struggle just to find enough to eat," I began. "Many people don't have simple necessities like a refrigerator, which only compounds their problems."

The governor nodded his head, but he didn't add anything to the conversation.

"Many of the people I help have to choose between food and medicine—a decision nobody should have to make. These are all hard-working people who simply can't make it without help."

For the duration of the meeting, the governor limited his responses. When he did offer something to the conversation, it was vague and non-committal. I had expected him to have researched the hunger problem in Alabama so that we could have an informed and meaningful conversation. When it was clear he hadn't, it became increasingly hard for me to concentrate. I started worrying about whether I had the right directions to get back onto Highway 29 to continue the walk to Washington.

I brought myself back to the conversation. It was obvious the governor had met with us to appease the public and get the media off his back. He had no interest in what we were saying. *Oh, well,* I thought. *Those who have ears to hear, let them hear.* I'm confident the President would have ears to hear—and eyes to read—my letter.

After our meeting, I stopped to talk to some reporters. I was kinder than I should have been about how it had gone. Sally Owens wrote an article that appeared in the *Mobile Press Register* explaining that I was walking to raise awareness about hunger and the death penalty. People started calling me on my mobile phone from all over the country to wish me luck. Some said they'd join us for part of the walk. At least some people were listening. Why was I surprised that the person to whom God had sent me—Governor Riley—was not among them?

A few people asked what I had against the death penalty. I challenged them to join me in walking the 900 miles to show just how much they believed in it. No one took me up on my challenge.

March 29: Waugh, Tysonville, and Shorter, Alabama

"What are you doing out here walking on this dangerous road?"

We were on a particularly beautiful stretch of Highway 84. Forget about the other side—the grass was greener on *this* side for a change! The roadsides were spotless. I hadn't come across any of my four-legged nemeses. And the sky was oh, so peaceful!

"I'm taking a stroll," I joked to Lucious Thomas, an elderly man sitting outside his house. He looked downright puzzled at the sight of me.

"Dangerous road," he said again.

"Going hungry is a lot more dangerous," I said. He shrugged.

"I'm walking 900 miles from Brewton all the way to Washington, DC," I continued. "I am going to personally deliver a letter to the President about the current state of the poor." I waited for his response.

He didn't seem to understand, or maybe I just didn't understand what he was asking. I gave him a big hug and told him he reminded me of my dad in his blue overalls. After another few miles, Frank and I stopped at a quaint-looking country shop. Adorable! If I hadn't known better, I might have thought I had trekked all the way up to Maine! Yes, it was that idyllic.

When I stepped inside the shop, I felt as if I had wandered onto another planet. The store was filled with all kinds of country fare. I asked the saleswoman the price of an item. She glared at me, but offered no response. I was interested in the darling items, so I asked again. Do you know what she did? Absolutely nothing. That was the weird thing. She turned her back on me and busied herself with a knickknack.

SCRANP!

The screen door to the shop ricocheted shut behind me. The sound gave me a jolt. I felt like a stray dog or cat that had been kicked out into the street. Frank sat in the van watching me. He didn't want to go into the country store—said it was too "cutesy" for him. I guess the woman thought the place was too cutesy for me, too.

The woman's "hospitality" made me feel dirty and contagious, as if I'd been injected with some lethal poison. My body felt limp, and though I walked on for about a mile, it didn't even feel like I was moving. I was in a mental fog. By the time I got to a bridge, my feet didn't even seem to touch the ground. It was all a blur.

It wasn't until my hands ran along the side rails of the rustic old bridge that I roused myself. Beneath the bridge was a noisy, babbling brook that sounded like it was gossiping. I placed my feet directly over the babbles and imagined the cool water was washing off the hurt.

Why was I exposing myself to this abuse? I searched my memory for a reason.

Oh, God, help us all remember that it is what is in one's heart that counts, not the color of one's skin, one's appearance, one's bank balance . . .

After a while a cool breeze refreshed me, and I was able to move on.

March 30: Tuskegee, Alabama

His hands were shaking. I was beginning to think that maybe he was a tad too old for this job. "We're almost at the next stop. Let's just get there."

His voice sounded curt. Upset. Walking had been pretty tough on me. But Frank? Remember, he was seventy-one. We had both underestimated the toll being my shadow driver would take. Most of the time he seemed frustrated and confused.

I picked up the pace so Frank could take a rest and imagined hiring a shadow driver for my shadow driver. Ha! How ridiculous would *that* look? People would think a parade—or a circus—was coming through town. We'd slow down traffic even more than we did already.

We made good time to Tuskegee. It was still early morning, and the dew on the grass glistened like candlewicks. Little birthday candles waiting to be lit for a celebration. I looked closer. Tiny insects were leaping from dewdrop to dewdrop, enjoying their morning refreshment.

As I marched into Tuskegee, my paths crossed with a hitchhiker whose day was just beginning. I gave him a start. I guess seeing the likes of me trudging along the highway was a stronger jolt than coffee.

"Car broke down?" he asked. I shook my head and nodded down the road toward Frank and the van. The hitchhiker asked the typical questions that most people did after reading the controversial signage.

"I don't get it. What are you doing?"

I explained what I was up to and what my goal was. The man's face puckered, like he had bitten into a lemon or something with an unexpected taste.

"How much they paying you to walk to Washington? They would have to pay me to walk that far."

This man thought I was raving mad. He thought my mission was bonkers. It seemed he was even trying to keep his distance from me. Like goodwill is infectious. Here's news for you all—goodwill *is* infectious!

At first his response irritated me. "They couldn't *pay* me to walk to Washington," I said. I continued on my way and allowed his comment to roll off my back. I had learned after many years that life is a lot easier without passing judgment. I chuckled, thinking I might even reach my destination first while the hitchhiker awaited his four wheels. Or maybe I'd see him drive past and wave before my day of walking was through. I was fine with either scenario.

The encounter made me smile. Why? I guess his comment had brought something about myself to light. I wouldn't have done this walk for any amount of money. I was walking for love. For humanity. And I was more deeply committed to this mission than even I had realized, primarily because I was deeply committed to the people I loved so dearly.

I continued my hike with renewed bounce. Farther along, a woman named Rhonda stopped and donated ten dollars. The donations were nice to get, and we could certainly use them, but what was more meaningful were the nice people reaching out to say hello and ask what I was doing. People like Rhonda and, yes, even that hitchhiker who thought I had a screw loose.

A bit farther on, I received a phone call from *The Brewton Standard*. They were checking in to see how the walk was going and what progress I'd made. A driver honked his horn as he drove past me. When I looked up and waved, the car was already vanishing from sight. I found out later that it was Florence Johnson and her family from Brewton, driving back home after attending a funeral in Tuskegee. It would have been nice if they'd stopped to say hello. That would have made my day.

As the day's walk came to a close, Frank's mood improved. My mood?

My mood had never been so good. I was counting my blessings, thanking God for giving me the opportunity to do His will and serve humanity. Sore legs and all.

If only others could taste the joy this was bringing me. If only they could experience the wonderful closeness to God that I was feeling—an intimacy that comes only when you trust Him and do His will.

Maybe this is what Jesus meant when He said, *"My food is to do the will of Him that sent me"* (John 4:34).

March 31: Auburn, Alabama

The way to Auburn was interrupted on and off by the occasional rainstorm. Frank and I made it to a shopping center around noon. It was time for lunch.

We chose a pizza place, which must have been the local Auburn teen hangout. As we ate our pizza, a group of twelve- to fifteen-year-olds eyed the van. They hesitated. Maybe they were shy? I could tell they were curious about what this was all about. I rolled down my window and invited them to come over and talk.

"All the way to Washington! Wow!" The kids were excited about my mission.

"When we see you on TV, we'll be able to say we met you!"

Sweet kids. Friendly and polite. One of them said she always complained about running a mile in PE, but she wasn't going to whine so much about it anymore. Ha! We discussed the issues, and the kids seemed genuinely concerned.

"We promise we'll watch you on TV if you meet the President!"

I thanked God for introducing me to the younger generation. I was filled with hope about the future. I had found in my travels that sometimes the greatest response came from the youth. For reasons I don't understand, adults often stop dreaming about how loving the world can be. They stop dreaming about the future and accept things as they are.

Frank called his ex-wife, Sharon, who came to meet us at a truck stop in Notasulga. She lived only about three miles away. She invited me to her home to take a well-deserved shower, but when I got there, I was shocked at the condition of her trailer. I almost fell through her bathroom floor! I gave her $150 of the money that had been donated to us to help her pay for repairs. Ah, so that's why God had sent Frank to me! It wasn't just to annoy me.

He knew Frank's ex-wife needed help and that I would have the means to do so, thanks to all the donations we'd been receiving. He had it all planned. Oh, God is good!

After my shower, Sharon dropped me back off at the truck stop so Frank and I could get a good night's sleep and an early start in the morning. It rained all night. It was one of the best night's sleep we'd had since starting the walk.

April 1: Happy Feet

Eleven days in, the unexpected happened! When I awoke that morning from a dreamy sleep, something had changed. My feet had gone through a kind of transformation. They were full of energy. I had happy feet!

Finally! My body had caught up to my mind and soul. It had adjusted to the walk and agreed to start cooperating with me on the journey. Not to complain here, but I still hadn't lost even a pound. You'd think after walking twenty miles a day for eleven days straight the fat cells would be trembling with worry. I thought at least a *few* of those interminable fat cells should have shrunk and disappeared by now.

Ah, well, nothing ever works out perfectly. And why should it?

More and more folks were hearing about my walk. God was sending curious folks to me who asked questions and were eager to discuss the hunger issue in America. The curious, the concerned, and the just plain friendly wanted to take time out to chat and wish us well.

Many people offered words of thanks. They were appreciative of the help they had received or grateful for non-profits that had helped those they loved. "If it wasn't for Meals on Wheels," one man told us, "my mother wouldn't be able to survive."

Something wonderful happens when you are a messenger for God. Your goodwill precedes you and you have friends everywhere—even in cities you've never visited before.

Of course, the rain wasn't about to stop for me. On my way to Lanett, it started pouring cats and dogs—and not the friendly ones. The weather got so bad that I had to look for cover. I couldn't find a place to duck inside fast enough, and in the process I got absolutely drenched. I looked like the boxing promoter Don King with my wet hair. I couldn't help but wonder if this was some kind of April Fools' joke.

Frank and I had made arrangements to spend the night at an anti-death-penalty activist's house in Lanett. It had been a while since I'd slept in a real bed. As I tried to fall asleep, all I could think about were the homeless folks who seldom had the opportunity to sleep under a roof, let alone in a bed.

Oh, God, thank You for all Your blessings. Give us all the love to share them fairly.

April 2: Lanett, Alabama

I couldn't exactly call the previous night's rest "beauty sleep." I awoke still looking like Don King, albeit a very tired Don King. Frank and I were hungry and ready for a good meal. One thing I'd learned on this walk was to be in the moment and thank God for what I had each day.

Before leaving Lanett, a supporter invited us to meet with her at city hall. I wasn't sure why she wanted the meeting, but we went anyway. When I arrived, I found the building was empty. I thought perhaps I had gotten the date wrong—or maybe she couldn't make it because of the rain? There wasn't a soul there except for Frank and me. The rain let up, and we were thinking about getting on our way when a couple of supporters from Vashon trickled in.

"I've heard all about you, Lisa," an elderly woman chimed. "Thank you so much for what you're doing!" She gave me a big bear hug. I turned around and noticed more supporters arriving. There were folks from all over—Vashon, Washington, and Montgomery counties. They led us into a reception hall, where Frank and I were greeted with singing, speeches, prayer, and, later in the day, a delicious home-cooked meal. What a contrast from how I had felt just an hour earlier! We had been running on empty, and now, what a miracle!

The reception came to a close, and I was anxious to get back on the trail. The supporters surprised us with $203.12 in donations. Why bother counting the cents? Because every bit meant so much. We desperately needed the money to compensate for the money I'd given to Frank's ex. The remaining money would be our food and gas money for the next few days. Oh, to be stable again. What a great feeling!

Better yet, we were only a few miles from the Georgia state line! Judy Cumbee from Lanett joined me as I walked my last few miles in Alabama. I hopscotched from Alabama into Georgia, giggling like I was twelve again. It was a milestone. Hurrah!

Then the Georgia welcoming committee arrived. In the form of a young policeman. "Ma'am, what are you up to?" he sighed. He looked bored.

"We're walking to bring light to the hunger issue in America," I said with extra oomph. The reception in Lanett had given me renewed vigor. "I'm also inviting people to reconsider the death penalty, because only God has the right to take a life."

The young policeman said we were fine as long as we didn't disrupt traffic.

"YAYYYYYYY! Way to go!" A car filled with teenagers pulled over, cutting off the policeman mid-sentence. They gave us all the money the four of them had—$1.04!

I think even the young policeman cracked a smile. We moved along.

CHAPTER THREE

Georgia

APRIL 3, 2005–APRIL 18, 2005

April 3: Georgia on My Mind

As I walked into Georgia, admiring the beauty of God's earth, I was thankful for not being stuck in a car. I never realized how much I missed as I sped along the highway. I marveled at the Georgia-green grass and the Georgia-blue lakes. So much of Georgia would have been lost on me if I simply zoomed by, peering through the windshield.

Hello, Georgia! I'm Lisa, and I am so happy to see you!

I was giddy. It was Day 13, after all. It was a dream come true to admire the beauty of nature without the interference of mankind. I crossed a bridge that sat over a lake and blew kisses at cute Georgia turtles floating in the water. How lucky I was!

My niece Wynter and her husband, Tovokious, joined me on my walk for a few hours. For lunch, Frank and I returned to Lanett to eat with one of our supporters. Good food tastes so much better after you feel like you earned it. Experiencing the lows—the discomfort of walking, my sore feet, feeling lonely—only made the highs that much richer. Food, friends, and nature. I felt so lucky my mind was with God, clear and open to appreciate life's bounty.

Lord, why did You choose me to do this?

"Because I knew you would do it," He answered.

Hah! If everyone were willing, everyone would be chosen. As tired as my feet were, it felt like I was on a cushion that was gently pushing me down the road. I walked on, still reveling in the beauty of my surroundings.

Oh, Lord, all Your children crave the beauty of Your creation. Show us how to make their world more beautiful.

April 4: La Grange, Georgia

When the dog went running scared with her tail between her legs, I should have recognized God's theme for me today: hospitality.

My first checkpoint was La Grange. I strolled through town, wary of the aggressive dogs as always, and heard quick-paced paw steps behind me. I turned and spotted a dog running after me, as if she were going to give chase. She almost got me running, but then I noticed her tail wagging the doggie version of "hello." I extended my hand into the air, but for some reason she took off running in the other direction.

I felt terrible. Here this sweet dog just wanted to greet me. She was showing a bit of Southern hospitality. Heck, let's call her my first furry supporter. But here I was scaring her off. What an ogre. When was I going to get over this phobia?

Judy Cumbee, whom we had met back in Lanett, arranged places for Frank and me to sleep for the night. Frank stayed with Judy and her husband, Bob, while I stayed with Judy's friends: Sam, Laura, and their two children, Sarah and Scottie.

Southern hospitality is no joke. Judy and her friends treated us to an old-fashioned barbecue with all the trimmings. We relaxed out back as they grilled hamburgers, made potato salad, tossed a refreshing green salad, and served some good old Southern sweet tea.

The welcoming atmosphere made me think wistfully of my own family back in Brewton. I missed my friends and family. At the same time, it was refreshing to be with people who treated us like family or old friends, even though we had just met.

The family donated twenty-five dollars to Carlisa, Inc. and set it up so that Sam's company would triple that. Before Laura went to bed, she prepared a breakfast casserole for me to eat the next morning. She asked me what time I was getting up and set the timer on the stove.

As I drifted off to sleep, I thought about the dog that had greeted me earlier. She was just being hospitable. After all, it's the Georgia way!

Whatever you do for the least of my little ones . . . oh, Lord, may they have abundant rewards in the kingdom of heaven.

April 5: Hogansville, Georgia

Georgia hospitality doesn't sleep. The smells of a delicious breakfast casserole made its way from Laura's oven and into my nostrils. Waking up at 6 AM was never so easy. Someone ought to invent a breakfast casserole alarm clock!

When I reconvened with Frank, I was pleased to hear he had also been treated to a breakfast alarm clock at Judy and Bob's house. With our bellies full, Frank and I drove to yesterday's stopping point to begin the next leg.

While the typical day on this journey was an adventure, today's events made it feel like a fairytale. As I meandered through breathtaking Georgia, I noticed different kinds of coins scattered along the highway. Some of them were new, while others looked like they hadn't moved in years. Often the placement of the coin made it seem as if somebody had deliberately put it on the road just for me!

Speaking of fairytales, I hoped this walk wouldn't end like that Hansel and Gretel story. Hansel and Gretel left breadcrumbs in the forest so they could find their way back home, but some forest critters came along and ate the breadcrumbs up. Hansel and Gretel were lost until that wicked witch found them. I couldn't remember . . . did the kids escape from the witch's gingerbread house at the end, or did the witch eat them up? As I moved along, picking up my coins (well, they were mine now—finders keepers, after all), I tried to remember what happened at the end of that old fairytale.

There were times as I walked deeper into Georgia, and farther away from home, when I definitely felt at my loneliest. I was beginning to feel abandoned by the folks back home. Nobody seemed to be making the effort to check in with me. Why was no one calling? I consoled myself in the fact that God had a plan for me and that those feelings of loneliness would pass. I just needed to stay focused. I imagined the trail of copper treasures was God illuminating His path for me.

"Thou wilt show me the path of life: in thy presence is fullness of joy; at thy right hand there are pleasures for evermore" (Psalm 16:11).

Five miles shy of Newman, I hit my twentieth mile for the day. Judy arranged for us to stay with a friend of hers. I chuckled, again reminded of Hansel and Gretel. Was Judy's friend going to invite us into a gingerbread house and cook *us* for dinner?

Judy's friend was no evil old witch. His name was Brad. When Frank and I arrived, he greeted us warmly. There was food, and fortunately it wasn't us! Brad cooked a tasty and nutritious meal. After dinner, we sat in his backyard and gazed at the stars. How amazing this day had turned out to be! The three of us chatted and kept company with his dogs (they were friendly too). It was magical.

The sky was vast, the stars numerous. I felt proud that we had made it this far and was grateful that total strangers had taken a chance and shared their homes with us. Of course, I still had pangs of homesickness, but God was connecting us with many friendly souls along the way who treated us like family.

The wine Brad kept pouring into my glass made me forget all my troubles. When I finally retired for the night, my bed seemed to be floating in the air. I remembered the ending to the fairytale. Hansel and Gretel fooled the witch and escaped her gingerbread house. It was a happy ending after all. Finally, I fell asleep.

Thank You, Lord, for giving us wine to "maketh glad the hearts of man" (Psalm 104:15).

April 6: Newman, Georgia

Today was the first day I was ready to turn back home. For real. I was nearly halfway through my day's walk when I looked up to see Frank making a wrong turn. Aaaaargh! What was he doing? Did he want me to drop dead of exhaustion?

I had to put the walk on hiatus and turn back to find him. After a three-mile detour, I finally located him. I was beyond tired, and I still had ten miles more to walk that day. And what did Frank have to say for himself? Nothing! Not even an apology! I turned into Carrie from the *Rocky Horror Picture Show*. I was fuming.

"Isn't it enough that I have to walk twenty miles a day? Now you have to add a few more on just for good measure! #@$%! What's the matter with you? You're supposed to be following me, not the other way around! You need to get your #@$% act together!"

"Heeeheheheeeeeeeeee!"

I swiveled backward to locate the source of the laughter. I was ready to knock someone out.

A little boy was standing in his yard, witness to my entire explosion (expletives and all). It cracked him up. Amid the guffaws, he pointed at Frank and cooed, "You went the wrong way, man." And then Frank started laughing, too. I wanted to cry.

I climbed into the van, and Frank drove me back to where I'd stopped. Now that I was back on track, I started walking the right way, huffing and puffing.

I mean, really, God. Was this the best You could do? This walk is hard enough as it is. Do I really need all these obstacles?

When we got to the truck stop that night, it started pouring rain. The van leaked all night. We were soaked.

Noah at least had an ark. I bet there were no leaks in that construction. They built things to last back then. And I'm stuck here in this van with Frank, of all people. Just me and him. It sounds like a tsunami is swelling outside.

I fought back my tears, just barely. I was destroyed. Scratch that. I was just feeling sorry for myself.

Thank You, Lord, for giving me a taste of the sufferings so many of Your poor endure daily. Thank You for reminding me of what they go through so I can feel compassion for them.

April 7: College Park, Georgia

Today my journey included a walk down memory lane in College Park, Georgia. (Note to self: I need to keep my expectations in check before embarking down such paths of nostalgia). College Park had been my old stomping ground in the mid-70s. Now, thirty years later, I didn't recognize it.

Frank and I were low on supplies, so we decided to shop at a local store. Just when Frank had found the perfect parking spot, a security guard joined us. And he wasn't laying out the red carpet. He had read the signs on our van.

"Excuse me," he said. "You can't park here."

"Why?" I said, confused. "We're going to shop here."

"You can shop here, but you can't park here," was his reply. He motioned to the signage on our van, as if the explanation for why we couldn't park was self-evident. We shut our doors and reversed.

Ugh. Our signs might be controversial, but they certainly aren't offensive. Where was the compassion? The negativity only made me want to throw in the towel again. Then I reminded myself of how things were when I lived in College Park. When I worked as a waitress, the racial prejudices I experienced were unspeakable. Yes, this small Georgia town had changed—the buildings, the roads, and the stores. But unfortunately, the people and their distorted ideas hadn't changed at all.

When I walked through most towns, I would ask myself if I could live there. Just for fun, you know? I'd say, "Lisa, would this be a town you might move to, if you wanted a change of scenery? Could you live here?" But College Park wasn't one of 'em. Been there, done that. Moved on.

Life has a way of surprising us. God shakes things up from time to time, maybe so we don't get bored and think we know everything. Ha! In our case, just a bit farther up the road, Frank and I encountered a glimmer of hope in the form of a kind man named Aaron. He invited us into his home, made us lunch, and donated twenty dollars.

I was about to ask, "Surely, you weren't born in College Park," when Aaron bolted up. Frank had dozed off in his recliner.

"Oh, no, you can't sleep here," he said. Poor old Frank! He was so tired. Aaron was a generous man, but he wasn't about to throw any slumber parties.

But, as Leonard Cohen sings, *"Oh the sisters of mercy, they are not departed or gone."* They were ready to throw us a slumber party. Okay, not really—I'm just joking. In fact, Sister Mary Magdala Thompson (1923–2012), of The Sisters of Mercy in Mobile, called and gave us a contact near Atlanta where we could spend the night. This saved us from another night of sleeping at a truck stop. Sister Magdala was a tireless advocate for social justice, and she was doing all she could to help us succeed. Our contact, Sister Pat, invited us to stay in her condo not far from the walking route.

After we arrived at Sister Pat's and got cleaned up, we were feeling relaxed and wondering what to have for dinner. Sister Pat's roommate recommended a place where we could find some good soul food. Talk about mercy! It was a refreshing change from all the fast food. Oh, what a blessing to be able to eat food you really love!

The whole time I was there, though, my mind was preoccupied. The road was long ahead . . .

April 8: The Sisters of Mercy

Sister Pat and I were up early to watch the Pope's funeral. Although she was going out of town, she prepared breakfast and left us a key so we could spend another night. What kindness! Of course, we didn't know if the neighbors agreed. The signs on the van attracted a lot of attention—a lot of lookie-loos. People loitered around the van and others drove by real slow, as if they were admiring Christmas lights.

We drove back to where we'd stopped walking the day before and carried on toward Atlanta. But once again, good ol' Frank went the wrong way . . . HOO, BOY! The traffic in Atlanta was a nightmare. I told him that because I was walking downtown he could just pull up somewhere out of the way. He caught some *zzzzzzzzs*.

Several workers greeted me when I marched past Catholic Social Services. Simone Blanchard, Sister Joyce Ann Hertziz, Tracey Klemone, and Jim Powers walked with me for several blocks. They were thrilled that someone was walking for hunger and the abolishment of the death penalty. It felt wonderful having their company and support. Plus, I got a T-shirt! The group presented me with a Catholic Worker T-shirt and thanked me for my commitment.

Frank went to bed early when we got back to Sister Pat's house. I couldn't sleep, so I busied myself with her reading material. Insomnia worked in my favor, as I came across a quote often cited by Mother Teresa. Ultimately, it became an enormous source of inspiration for me during the rest of my journey.

People are often unreasonable and self-centered. Forgive them anyway.
If you are kind, people may accuse you of ulterior motives.
Be kind anyway.
If you are honest, people may cheat you.
Be honest anyway.
If you find happiness, people may be jealous.
Be happy anyway.
The good you do today may be forgotten tomorrow.
Do good anyway.
Give the world the best you have, and it may never be enough.
Give your best anyway.
In the end, it is between you and Him, not you and them.[1]

---

1   Dr. Kent M. Keith, "The Paradoxical Commandments," originally published as part of a booklet for student leaders in 1968.

April 9: Atlanta, Georgia

Today we would wrap up our time in Atlanta. The traffic was still a nightmare, and Frank couldn't find a place to park. I told him that he could park farther ahead than usual and we'd rendezvous later.

As I walked through town, I crossed paths with a man sitting on a bench. "Excuse me, miss," he said. "Do you have a dollar to spare?"

"What can you buy for a dollar in Atlanta?" I asked. It seemed like a fair question. He smiled.

"Not much, but I'm hoping I'll be able to get money from others. I'm just trying to collect enough for a cup of coffee and some food."

"What's your name?"

"Ryan."

"Nice to meet you, Ryan. My name is Lisa. I was just about to eat lunch. Would you like to join me?" I could see a good-looking place up the street.

We finished our food and had a cup of coffee together. I was curious how Ryan ended up on the streets.

"I used to work at a restaurant," he said, "but I was hardly making enough money. I could barely pay for rent, utilities, and food. I got laid off a year ago and had nothing to fall back on. Without a job, I had no way of holding down a place. So I turned to the streets."

"What about your family?"

"My parents live in New Jersey. I haven't spoken to them in a few years. They have no idea I'm living on the streets."

I shared my story of being homeless in Los Angeles during my twenties. "I felt ashamed," I revealed to Ryan. "I still haven't told my family."

"I'll get back on my feet," he said. "It won't be long from now."

Before Ryan and I parted ways, we gave each other a hug. "Goodbye, Ryan," I said. "Here's a little something to help you out. I hope it does."

I gave him fifty dollars. It was a miniscule amount considering the enormous challenges he faced, but it was all I could manage. As I continued my walk, I thought about Ryan and the plight of the homeless. Why must those who struggle feel so much shame? The true shame comes from those in the community who have the means to help but choose not to do so.

As I've gotten older, I've begun to understand why some people show compassion and others don't. I really can't fault those who don't, as it comes down to personal experience. Struggling, living on the streets, going hungry—those are issues that many people haven't encountered, so it remains abstract to them. To truly help Ryan, the community has to come together and help one another. Until that happens, people in situations similar to Ryan's will continue to struggle.

I suddenly realized why this walk was meaningful to me and the many communities I'd marched through so far. I now knew why I absolutely had to finish it. It was because *results only happen through action.* As others witnessed my walk, or heard about my mission to Washington, DC, it built awareness. Those who haven't experienced poverty would now be more likely to admit that the problems of hunger and capital punishment were a reality.

That was why I had to finish the walk.

I prayed God would help people rediscover their true humanity—to become the people He had called them to be. I thought Bryant McGill put it eloquently when he wrote in an online article:

> *True progress for humanity is anything that takes us closer to supporting one another. Small acts of kindness between you and the individuals around you are the germination that springs into being something as mysterious as life itself, and what may in fact be humanity's greatest accomplishment—compassion for others. Let us all strive to cultivate a deeper and more meaningful desire to ease the burdens of others. Every person is a precious gift, and we are all like little children who yearn for acceptance, safety and unconditional love. Let us all reach out with a hope that we could each bring some degree of happiness to other human beings. Let each of us lead a revolution of support in the lives of others.[2]*

That evening, Frank and I returned to Sister Pat's home and enjoyed more time with the nuns. It felt amazing to be in the warm embrace of like-minded people. If only folks would learn to live for one another instead of themselves, the communities outside the nunnery would experience the warmth and compassion I was feeling right then.

April 10: God Bless SAS Shoes!

Frank and I got an early start and hit the road at 5:30 AM. As I walked, a car

---

2   Dr. Kent M. Keith, "The Paradoxical Commandments," originally published as part of a booklet for student leaders in 1968.

zoomed past, did an abrupt U-turn, and circled back to me.

"Are you afraid people might see the signs and act violently toward you?" the driver asked. I peered into the car as the window rolled down.

"I'd be more afraid if I didn't take the walk and help people learn about the major hunger problem in America," I said. "I'd be more afraid if innocent people on death row were executed. So, no, I'm not afraid that people will act violently toward me."

The window rolled further down, revealing a kind woman offering five dollars. "I wish I could contribute more," she said, "but God will bless you for walking against the death penalty. I'll pray for your safety, though after speaking with you I don't think you'll need it."

I smiled as the woman peeled off.

Frank and I stopped to fill up at a gas station, and I took a poke around. I was so glad I did! Would you believe it? Inside the store, there was a one-dollar radio just sitting there, waiting for me. This day was turning out A-Okay.

Not only did I have music to keep me occupied on the walk, but also the shoes SAS had donated were proving to be a dream. I felt like I was floating rather than walking. Of course, the shoes weren't the only support I had—I had to give credit to the Father, Son, and Holy Spirit for walking with me and keeping me from getting tired.

God also introduced me to a local named Susan. She bought us lunch and shared how distressed she was about the increasing number of families who needed help in her community. "I'm so glad people are beginning to recognize there is a hunger problem in our country," she said.

Of course, there are two sides to everything, and today was no exception. Although we were received with a heartwarming amount of positivity and acceptance, we also encountered the usual mood dampeners. When we marched into Haynesville, a friend called to check on me and said that no one would blame me if I cut my trip short and turned around. What's the deal? Why wouldn't I follow through on my walk? After all, I'd come this far, hadn't I?

Words of encouragement were what I really throve on right then. *Oh ye of little faith. When would they get it?*

April 11: Haynesville, Georgia

The day started out wonderful. I found a treasure on the street in Haynesville—a necklace with the inscription, *"Be strong and courageous. Do not be discouraged or terrified."* I took this message as the words of encouragement I'd been craving.

I fell back on this message later that day when the van broke down. Frank was scared. I was scared. We were broke. I called AAA, and they said a tow truck was on the way. Two seconds later, Frank was so panicked about the breakdown that he flagged down the first tow truck he saw! I was too slow on my sore, tired feet.

I should have asked the driver if he was from AAA. When we arrived at the shop, we found out he wasn't. He towed us seventeen miles, and the bill was $80! I was so mad at Frank and myself. When AAA called trying to find us, they were pretty upset as well.

Well, this venture wasn't promised to be a walk in the park. Trials and tribulations were part of the package in every walk of faith. Especially this one. Ha!

All kidding aside, my faith was rattled when the mechanic told us it would cost $500 to fix the van. In addition, the repairs would delay our walk by a day. The heat and air condenser needed fixing. It hurt terribly, but I would have to write a check and pay for the repairs. I thanked God I had the money in the bank to pay.

We called it a day, and Frank joined me on a walk down the highway to find a room for the night. It was funny seeing Frank without a steering wheel in front of him.

April 12: A Dozen Thanks

Instead of counting sheep, I counted dollar bills. I couldn't sleep. The van, the pricey repairs, how much this trip was costing—SNORRRRRR-REEEEEEEEEE!

"Frank, roll on your side," I said. "You're snoring!" He didn't hear me. At least someone was resting easy!

A story came on the news about a nun named Sister Barbara. She had been killed in Argentina trying to help a tribe save their land. What was my problem? Here was a person who had given her life for what she believed in, and I was worried about a heater or air condenser or whatever repair. I felt ashamed. *Okay, Father. I hear You.*

Still, I had to admit that despite the guilt, it was a long, worrisome walk back to the garage. Money was a big concern when pulling off a walk such as this. *But again, it's a trivial thing,* I thought. *Stop complaining, Lisa.*

Surprise, surprise! The mechanic had learned about my mission and decided to charge me only $209! He believed in what we were trying to do and figured out another way to complete the work at a cheaper price. Looking for negotiation tactics with your mechanic? Set course on a walk for fifty days, and they may bend on the price. Whatever works! I thanked the mechanic for his generosity at least a dozen times and gave him a hug. I thanked God, too. This trip had been full of surprises.

We loaded up and headed back to the place we'd stopped the day before. Finally, I would be able to resume the walk! Oh, why did I keep forgetting that God had everything under control? My mood was light and free, a perfect combination. Even with the late start, I managed to walk almost ten miles. We stayed at a rest area that night. I slept peacefully.

April 13: Seventeen Gloves and a Bra

Today I followed another kind of breadcrumb trail, only it wasn't old coins but a trail of gloves. And a bra for good measure!

The weather didn't look too promising, so Frank and I decided to start our twenty-third day a little earlier than usual. Counting the gloves kept me occupied—I didn't dare pick them up and collect them. After just a few miles, I counted seventeen gloves, and none of them had a mate! I guess gloves suffer from that same sock problem you encounter after when you wash them. You always lose the better half.

Most of the gloves were work gloves. The bra? I didn't even want to know how that wound up on the side of the road.

The van repairs resolved our stress, and we were happy to share in the good mood. I was a little too giddy—floating while walking on the highway is ill advised. A car nearly hit me because I was walking too close to the road. ROOOOOOOOOOOOARRRRRR!

Some sections of the highway were difficult to navigate, and I couldn't get off the road. Each time a big semi roared by, it almost blew me down with the wind! Most of the time, when a big truck passed, I'd stop and brace myself. Walking on the highway certainly wasn't for the faint of heart. It was dangerous and scary. We received many waves hello, and a few curses too, just to keep things interesting and down to earth. Odd thing? I felt safe. God had shown me I was going to be fine.

"Even though I walk through the valley of the shadow of death, I will fear no evil" (Psalm 23:4).

After four hours of treading along, we rested in a beautiful wooded area surrounded by tall pine trees. We ate lunchmeats, bread, and chips and drank some cold water. Ahh! It was a nice, cool place. Such relaxation! Frank and I enjoyed the peace in our dreams, too, as we dozed for a short nap.

"He maketh me to lie down in green pastures: he leadeth me beside the still waters. He restoreth my soul" (Psalm 23:2-3).

After our nap, I walked for another five miles. We spent that night in a gas station parking lot. Talk about variety on this journey!

April 14: Athens, Georgia

The streets grew narrow in Athens, which made my dog shuffling strategy moot. I ambled along, reflecting on a chat I'd had about the death penalty with a waitress in a small café whose boyfriend was in prison. Just then, two dogs ran out from behind a house. They were barking their heads off and coming . . . straight . . . for . . . me . . .

"Frank!" I yelled, my eyes darting around like a pinball machine. "Frannnkkkkkk!" Where was he?

I walked backward, retracing my steps down the street. I kept my walking stick outstretched in front of me, wielding it like a weapon. "Back off, you mutts. Don't take one paw closer, or I'll . . ."

The dogs either took my threat seriously or felt so sorry for my pitiful self that they backed off. I sprinted down the street, back to where Frank had dropped me off. *He is going to get a piece of my mind . . .*

I found him parked a ways back. Guess what? He was sound asleep in the van! What the heck was I paying him for?

"If you ever do that again and I get bitten," I said, "you won't be getting paid when we get back home! Are you outta your #@$% mind?"

"%#$@ no!" he said.

"You are the craziest #@$% I know," I said.

"Who can be any crazier than your @#$%?"

"Really?" I asked. I crawled into the van and took time to be alone. Frank walked circles alongside the highway. *Maybe I should drive and see how far he gets.*

Of course, we both settled down. Twenty minutes later, we were okay with each other again. That's what I liked about my relationship with Frank. We could get upset, but neither of us held a grudge. Ten minutes after arguing, we'd be laughing about something. I don't think this trip would have been bearable if I couldn't even talk to the only steady company I had.

As I continued my walk, a radio program hosted by actor-musician John Tesh came on and heightened my mood. What better soundtrack for a long walk than good music and great info? His music helped me escape my frustrations. He talked about a variety of things, from what to eat to why we ought to tip hotel maids. Apparently, maids were paid only five dollars a room. Goodness! It's as bad as being a waitress. Or a cotton picker!

I made a mental note to tip the maids generously the next time I stayed at a hotel. All too often we just don't realize what's going on in the lives of those who serve us. There are so many little acts of kindness we could perform if we just had eyes to see or ears to listen.

Lord, let us always be aware of our neighbor's needs.

April 15: Hounds from Hell

I had company today, and not the friendly kind. Just as we neared Athens, a state trooper, a sheriff, and a policeman stopped us—all within a five-minute time span!

Someone had called all three branches of the law to report a suspicious-looking vehicle in the area, and they wanted to make sure that we weren't going door-to-door soliciting donations. Some people have a lot of time on their hands, I guess. I can't imagine why anyone would call three branches of law enforcement because of the signs on the side of our van!

My furry fiendish friends greeted us in Athens, too. Two of them charged at me before I could devise a plan to avoid them. Then my angel, Frank, finally pulled through as my shadow driver! He even ventured out of his safety zone. He sprang out of the van with a stick and helped me fight them off. Good ol' Frank!

I was shaken up and had to lean beside the van for the next few minutes. When Frank and I got our bearings, we plodded on. Shortly afterward, I was feeling nostalgic for those canines. One of the two-legged kind passed me and threw a cup of ice in my face! Nice.

I kept losing service on my mobile phone as I walking on the highway.

What if I needed help? I did find another kind of help, though. In the middle of the highway, I noticed quarters, nickels, and dimes. It was as if the streets were covered in silver! It was like being on a treasure hunt, and I wound up collecting $1.58. Ha, ha!

"Thou preparest a table before me in the presence of mine enemies . . . my cup runneth over" (Psalm 23:5).

April 16: Commerce, Georgia

Six-pack of soda, CDs, a brand new gas can . . . just some of the new finds I discovered walking along the highway to Commerce. How did all this stuff end up here? I could plant myself on the side of the road and open a flea market. I really could. After all, I'd already found an assistant. You wouldn't believe it if I told you.

Okay, I'll tell you. A huge black Labrador greeted me on the road. Seeing that he was friendly, I took a moment to make his acquaintance. As I moved on my way, I noticed the dog was following me. I walked faster. So did the dog. I went right, and then left. So did the dog. He was on my tail like a magnet. I just couldn't seem to get rid of him. (I have that kind of effect on men. Ha!)

My furry companion refused to part from me. It got to a point where he was disrupting traffic. He'd tag along with me for a few yards, and then dart into the street when something caught his fancy, only to return to my side moments later. Meanwhile, the cars blared their horns at him.

"Crazy woman, get your dog!" People thought we were a pair! I was getting nervous my new sidekick was going to get crushed and become dog pâté. I had no choice but to turn around and walk the dog back to his house. This would be another day where I was doomed to walk more miles than my route required.

"Stay. STAY!" I said back at the dog's house, commanding him to stay on that porch. I said it in a really rude and threatening way. The dog was hurt; he thought I was his new family. Still, I was happy. This was how the world was supposed to be—all creatures great and small, friendly, helpful, and kind.

Even though it was a painful breakup, that dog gave me good luck. After my encounter with him, all the dogs I came across were friendly. Not that I'm a Pied Piper of dogs or anything—none of them followed me along the highway. But my dog phobia abated somewhat.

The dog must have had the magic touch on humans, too. Near Commerce, three people stopped to see if we needed help. They thought that maybe we'd broken down. One offered his mobile phone for me to use, and the other two asked if we needed a ride. Later, while we were having lunch at a restaurant, a man came over to our table, paid for our meal, thanked us for what we were doing, and said, "God bless."

April 17: Trains and Trucks

"Be careful, there isn't any dog ordinance in this area. Between the dogs and the people, this area can be kind of dangerous." I was getting a mouthful from a woman who stopped me in the street. "Just a few months ago I was attacked by one of my neighbor's dogs," she continued. "See?" She pointed out a "scar." Honestly, I couldn't see anything. I nodded and moved along. I resisted the urge to tell her, "Go away, oh bearer of bad news. Go away."

It was Day 27, and we were well on our way. Several people stopped me with kind words of encouragement. A woman named Carolyn thanked me and donated twenty dollars to the cause. Farther down the road, a man donated his last three dollars. "It's all I have," he said as he handed me the money." I wish I could give you more."

It was wonderful to be in a community where several of the citizens stopped to donate, whether they were donating their time by saying a quick hello or with money. Both were equally generous and appreciated.

Although I didn't see any vicious dogs, I told Frank that he wasn't allowed to venture more than a few feet away from me. I walked along trembling. The big black Labrador from yesterday hadn't been able to totally abate my fear of dogs, I guess. Old habits die hard. Ah well . . .

I needn't have worried. No ferocious dogs crossed paths with me that day. I did, however, encounter another fearsome enemy: loneliness.

I had a lot of time to think as I walked along this highway. Too much time, in fact. It could drive a person nuts! I couldn't imagine what the innocent men on death row experienced. God intended for human beings to be social and cooperate with others. That's our element. I'm sure of that now more than anything after encountering all the lovely people on my walk.

To prevent driving myself to insanity, I made it my business to find distractions. When we were walking next to train tracks and I heard a train coming, I'd run to the railroad crossing and wave at the conductor. He usually waved back, and I laughed as if I were ten years old. I did the same with the big trucks.

The connection to other travelers eased my solitude. Somewhat.

"Unless you become like one of these little ones . . . " (Matthew 18:3).

Yes, I was lonely. But I also found true meaning in what I was doing. And that brought pure bliss, even if I did have to sleep in a store parking lot again that night.

April 18: Bill Williams and the Sleeping Bags

I could see the state line all the way from where I was walking! I'd been dreaming about it. Visualizing it. And today was the day!

Bill Williams drove over from Birmingham to join me again. Together, we made it all the way to my second milestone, South Carolina! To celebrate, Bill took us out to dinner. And not fast food—it was REAL FOOD, with salad and everything! I even put a napkin in my lap and used silverware. Plastic sporks get old. This was a treat!

The weather was cooling off. Any day now, Frank and I would start shivering in the van (we didn't have any blankets). Bill planned to accompany me all day, but he had to cut his visit short when his car broke down so he could repair it. Before leaving us for the day, he bought us two sleeping bags and donated eighty dollars. Bless Bill.

We put those two sleeping bags to good use that night. It was chilly in the store parking lot. But I knew that with John Tesh on the radio and the warmth from Bill's sleeping bags, we'd be able to spend the night comfortably. I thanked God for both of them, as well as for the woman who stopped by the van and donated three dollars to help out with gas.

You might scoff at three bucks, but when gas money is scarce, every donation adds up. Oh, yes, all those little gestures added up to great joy!

CHAPTER FOUR

South Carolina

APRIL 19, 2005–APRIL 22, 2005

April 19: South Carolina

The three dollars donated yesterday was the precise amount we needed to park the van in a nature area for a much-needed break. The walk into South Carolina was breathtaking. After we parked, we wandered onto the beach. I gathered shells and enjoyed the sun and cool water. I tell you, someone could have shot a Club Med commercial of me luxuriating in the salty air. The respite felt like a vacation.

What did Frank do? Nap, of course! So I had the beach to myself. Not only did Frank refuse to join me on the beach, but other people also refused my company. Several parties drove by, ready to park, but when they saw the van on the beach, they immediately turned and wheeled out of there!

Jokes on them (suckers). This beach was gorgeous—and I could enjoy the solitude for a little while. *My dears, it might not have been your intention, but giving a girl some space can be a great gift too!*

Enough of the break. I got back to footing it and was blessed to see a beautiful lake. The water was translucent.

"How manifold are thy works, O Lord! In wisdom hast thou made them all; the earth is full of thy riches" (Psalm 104:24).

April 20: Anderson, South Carolina

A huge blue whale of a truck barreled straight at me today and tried to swallow me whole. I dodged out of the way just in time. At first I thought I was being careless, but when I glanced back at the two young white men driving and realized they were laughing, it became clear the incident was intentional.

I know walking on the highway involves the risk of getting hit by a car, but to be hit by a car *on purpose?* That was unthinkable. I was shaken up.

Some friends called me shortly afterward. "Lisa, you have to come back home." "Lisa, quit this walk business. Now is the time to STOP." "Lisa, the only difference you're going to make is getting yourself killed!" My friends hoped to bring me back to my senses and convince me to quit. Ha! I was more stubborn than they took me for. My determination was at its peak. I WOULD finish this walk, darn it.

Of course, I'd be on the lookout for more crazies as I continued.

That night we slept in a motel room in Anderson, South Carolina. I watched the movie *Crazy in Alabama.* I don't know why, but for some reason it made me feel better. Ah, Alabama. I missed home.

This room was damp and smelled like mildew. Thinking about it brought me down from the high of the movie. Frank was sleeping on the body pillow from the van. I was in the bed. He snored so much it was like having a herd of horses in the room. I hoped he wouldn't snore all night.

April 21: Greensville, South Carolina

Frank snored all night. When I finally did fall asleep, I dreamed I was a wild horse and a rancher had lassoed me. I woke up in a cold sweat screaming, "Neigh! Neigh!" Panicked, I look around the room. Frank was still snoring. Let this be a lesson to anyone out there who has some romantic notion about walking for a cause.

Needless to say, only one of us slept well.

Today I would walk to Greensville. It would have been great if some kind soul had walked ahead of me and mowed this side of the highway. The grass was up to my thighs! I had cars on one side and snakes on the other. How did I know about the snakes? Because I saw about a dozen dead ones on the road. I wondered if they'd had a run-in with that blue truck like I did—but weren't as lucky.

An elderly woman, who looked to be somewhere in her late seventies, stopped and donated twenty dollars. She also gave me a bottle of cold, sweet tea. I thanked her and told her I'd drink it when we got closer to a bathroom.

I think she understood why. Before parting ways, she said, "I'm so grateful for what you're doing. Poor folk need more people like you to stand up for them." I gave her a big hug.

If you're wondering why I accepted donations from people who seemed relatively poor—the very people I was supposed to be helping—the reason is actually quite simple. That spirit of giving was the very thing I was promoting.

Much of what I received I passed on to someone who really needed it. I generally kept only what I needed for myself and gave the rest away. Who knows, maybe we wouldn't even have needed money if everyone did his or her bit for free.

Frank and I took a break from the walk to eat in a nice little restaurant. A woman came in and sat at the table in front of me. She looked sad, and there was a message on her T-shirt that read, "Someone say something that will cheer me up." So, naturally, I bustled over to her like a bull in a China shop and offered my assistance, hoping that would cheer her up. She smiled and thanked me. All she really wanted was to chat with someone for a bit. Sometimes it really is just the thought that counts.

While having dinner the same day, Frank and I met another woman—a total stranger—who invited us to spend the night at her home. Even though we couldn't find her house and ended up staying in a parking lot again, it was heartwarming to know there were people out there like that woman supporting us in spirit.

April 22: Dogs on the Loose!

It had been a while since my last encounter with my four-legged enemies. April 22 marked the dog-day afternoon revival. That day I encountered not ONE, not TWO, but THREE dogs. Through a coordinated effort, the three beasts joined forces to harass me.

I didn't see them fast enough. In fact, by the time I was aware of them they had almost JUMPED me, growling fiercely. I wielded my trusty walking stick/dog weapon, but that only seemed to irritate them. Their choppers oozed with even more salvia. These guys tasted blood. My blood!

"FRANNNNNNNNNKKKKKK!"

I was terrified. I waved my stick at the dogs—and actually had to hit one of them when his fangs got too close. *What are these? Vampire dogs?*

Where the heck was their owner? My eyes were tearing up. Was this how it was all going to end? Being ripped to pieces by vicious mutts?

I finally made my way to the van. Frank got out to help me, but they were persistent. "I was almost dog food, Frank!" I said. "Where were you?"

"I'm sorry, Lisa. Hop in." He told me he would start to be more conscious of these four-legged beasts of prey.

Why doesn't South Carolina require dogs to be fenced in? That law needs to be put in place. The possibility of meeting up with all kinds of mutts, especially pit bulls, was truly scary! Why couldn't a person feel free to walk past a house without worrying about being attacked?

Please, Lord. Don't send me on another walk to fight for dogs being leashed.

North Carolina

APRIL 23, 2005–MAY 2, 2005

April 23: Belmont, North Carolina

"Beeeep! Beeeeep!" Finally, my mobile phone was working again! I started getting reception as I headed into Belmont on Route 29. I thanked God that I was never in a situation where I had to call for help.

An hour later, I was nostalgic for when I *didn't* have reception. Dozens of people were calling to wish me well, but their caller ID was blocked. I guess they were scared I'd call them back. I mean, really! Did they think I was going to call them and ask for money or something? Or did they think I'd tell on them? Cowards! I finally decided to stop answering the phone if I couldn't see who was calling.

On the other hand, a few people who had offered to help me with a place to stay didn't answer their phones. Ha! Maybe I should have blocked *my* caller ID. Maybe then they would have answered! In any case, I was perfectly content staying in the van, so it wasn't necessary for them to make idle offers. All they had to do was call and say hello, good luck, and God bless, not make offers they couldn't keep.

I took Sister Magdala's advice and asked the Pope to stand on my right side and Jesus on my left. At times when I felt worn out, I could actually feel them lifting me up and helping me along.

"Do not judge lest you be judged yourselves" (Matthew 7:1).

April 24: Sisters of Mercy Convent

I was walking to Belmont today. I checked several times to see if anyone from home had called. Why didn't I hear from them?

Once we reached Belmont, Sister Magdala from Mobile arranged for Frank and me to stay at the Sisters of Mercy Convent. Move over, Hilton. I thought I had died and gone to heaven! What a beautiful place! The grounds were landscaped with sweet-smelling flowers. Everything had its own place.

There were thirty nuns, including one who was visiting from Africa. They ran a shelter on the grounds that housed families in need and victims of domestic abuse. We toured the dorms where the families lived and discovered there was also a school. The nuns invited us to stay for two nights. I'm so glad we accepted! We were treated like royalty. Each of us received our own suite to stay in, which was located in a huge dorm-like building. The suite had its own kitchen, bedroom, living room, and bathroom.

And get this: a cook prepared meals. Each day we were treated to wonderful food prepared by great cooks. Yum!

We attended evening mass with the sisters. That night, they slipped a donation of $195 under my door. It was a nice surprise! Of course, I was still missing home and wished my family would give me a call to check-in, but it was certainly nice to feel so welcomed here with the Sisters.

Walking with the Lord, you are always with family.

April 25: A Day Off!

We took the day off, relaxed, and spent some time with the sisters. While we were sitting on the porch, a huge turtle came up to the patio. It seemed fascinated by us all. The sisters had never seen it before. The turtle must have felt the warm energy of the place because it stayed with us until late afternoon.

Frank and I washed our clothes, cleaned out the van, and got everything ready for the next day. We joined the sisters for devotion. Later in the evening, we enjoyed watching TV and relaxing in our rooms. It was a wonderful and much-needed break! Now, if I could only hear from the folks back home.

Thank You, Lord, for providing us with Your wonderful bounty of food and shelter.

April 26: Help, Thieves!

I was up at 5 AM. It was easy for me to rise so early after a day of R & R. Now it was back to R & R & R & R (road and road and road and road . . .)

Before setting off, we enjoyed a glorious breakfast with the Sisters. When it was time for us to leave, they said a special prayer for us. They also gave us supplies from their food closet (juice, drinks, and snack food.) We exchanged big hugs and loaded up the van. I started my walk straight out of the convent's gate while Frank wheeled in the van behind me. As I looked up at the sky and felt the pleasant breeze, I knew straight off it was going to be a great day for walking.

In the middle of the day, a woman called to invite us to her home near Charlotte, North Carolina, to spend the night. But when the time came to get directions, I couldn't get her on the phone. Not sure what happened there. After I had completed my twenty miles, Frank and I started looking for a place to sleep for the night.

It was getting dark. Luckily, we found a possibility on a back road. Sure, it was a little isolated and scary, but we needed to find a place before it got much darker.

"Can we park our van and sleep here, sir?" Frank and I asked a manager at the local gas station.

"Certainly, just park right around back," he replied. "You won't be disturbed, and you'll profit from a good night's rest."

By midnight we were sleeping quietly. Well, you know what I mean by *quietly*—me, Frank, and his herd of horses! The herd didn't wake me up, though. It was the loud KNOCK on the van window that did. After struggling a bit with the window lock, I opened it and found two men standing there. They identified themselves as policemen.

The policemen were joined by another store manager—the one who had earlier given us permission to park was no longer there. The new staffers had noticed the van in the back and called the police to report someone trying to break into the store.

We cleared up the misunderstanding, and it all worked out. Thank goodness the policemen weren't gun-happy. The night manager was upset that the evening manager hadn't told him about us. We went into the store and talked to the workers, but the experience left me feeling a little violated.

Oh, God, is this a small taste of how Your children feel when they are wrong-

fully convicted of a crime? Comfort them, Lord, and wash them clean in the fire of Your love.

April 27: Lost

We ran into a snag the next morning when we left the gas station parking lot. The signs pointing back to the highway were confusing as heck! "Frank, how did we end up on the wrong highway?" I asked.

Of course, I couldn't blame him. The back roads were like a labyrinth. It took us almost an hour to find our way back to our starting spot. Once we did, I was happy to get out of the van and start moving. By the end of the day, I had completed a wonderful twenty-one mile walk, mostly on open road. There weren't many houses, and the weather was just right. Many people honked their horns in support.

My shoes were reaching their limit. When I first started the hike, they squeaked like baby chicks. Now the soles were worn thin, and I hadn't heard a squeak from them in twenty-five days. My feet were feeling more tired. I kept switching the insoles, hoping to make them last a little longer. It seemed to help.

Frank and I spent the night in another store parking lot. It was well lit, so we felt safe and slept well. I learned a valuable lesson that day: anybody can make a wrong turn and get lost or turned around. I had to be careful what I fussed about and choose my battles on this walk.

Thank You, God, for Frank's easygoing personality.

April 28: Salisbury, North Carolina

"Another airplane. Another sunny place. I'm lucky, I know. But I wanna go home. Mmmm, I've got to go home."

That was the second time I'd heard that song that day. Michael Bublé's "I Wanna Go Home" was definitely a long-running theme of this walk. My homesickness was becoming more and more difficult to ignore. I really missed my mom and dad. I wished I could hear from my family. But I knew the only sure way to see them was to finish the walk, because there was no way I'd be quitting early—homesickness or no homesickness! The only thing that could stop me were my feet.

I called SAS shoes and asked if they would donate a pair of insoles. The woman who answered my call was named Rebecca, and she complied with my request. I didn't have any address to receive mail, let alone a package, so I asked them to send the insoles to my friend Jack Payden-Travis's house. Jack lived in Virginia, where he served as the director of Virginians for Alternatives to the Death Penalty. He, more than anyone else we'd met along the way, had become really involved in our walk.

Along the way, a policeman stopped me and warned that Frank was pulling too far ahead to be able to help me out if I needed it. He suggested that I tell him to park a bit closer. When I finally got to Frank, I scolded him and warned him again about leaving me so far behind. I was tired of having to tell him about it. Maybe he was hard of hearing, but I'm certain he heard me that time.

I shuffled off in a huff. Later, Tim McGraw's song, "Live Like You Were Dying," came on the radio.

> *Skydivin',*
> *I went rocky mountain climbin',*
> *I went 2.7 seconds on a bull name Fumanchu.*
> *And I loved deeper,*
> *And I spoke sweeter,*
> *And I watched an eagle as it was flyin'.*
> *And he said someday I hope you get the chance,*
> *To live like you were dyin'.*[1]

As I stood on that street corner in Salisbury, it dawned on me that I was doing exactly what the song said: I was living like I was dying. It was an incredible feeling! I realized that this was my dream. I couldn't expect everyone to share it, but that didn't make me feel any less lonely.

Bless Frank, Lord. Of all the quirky things that he does, none are done with malice.

April 29: It's Raining Wieners!

We got a ten-mile break when Highway 29 turned into an interstate and the local police told us we couldn't walk on it. I felt like I was cheating until

---

1   Tim McGraw, "Live Like You Were Dying," from Live Like You Were Dying (Nashville, TN: Curb Records, 2004).

God said to me, "Ten miles are only ten miles. Take your blessings and be grateful."

Frank's driving was getting worse. He was nervous, and his hands shook on the steering wheel. One man actually gave us the elbow instead of the finger because of Frank's slow driving. Didn't Frank realize you have to drive faster than twenty miles per hour on the interstate? *I could walk faster than he drives. Golly.*

We reached the place where the interstate turned back into Highway 29 and I could resume the walk. I went by a lot of houses with dogs. Frank and I came up with the idea of putting hotdog wieners in my pocket so when a dog came at me, I could throw the wieners to distract it.

When it actually came down to testing the theory, the dogs looked so vicious and my hands were shaking so badly that I threw the whole pack at them and took off running. When I looked back, it was raining wieners! But the plan worked—it distracted the dogs long enough for me to make it farther down the road. With my heart pounding in my chest, I was finally able to sit down and take a rest.

Oh, Lord, You said we should bless those who curse us. It also seems to be a good idea to bless those who want to eat us.

April 30: Foot Soldier

As of today, I have a new moniker. Eric J.S. Townsend, a reporter for the *Greensboro News and Record,* nicknamed me "Foot Soldier." That was his title for the piece he wrote about my walk. Townsend had spotted the van and asked if he could do a story on our cause. It only took me about a millisecond to respond.

"YES! Of course. Can we walk and talk?"

The day was rainy, but it was the type of rain you could walk in. Townsend joined me for a bit, taking pictures and asking questions about our cause.

I explained to him that if just one innocent person is sitting on death row, the system needs to be abolished. There is no way it can be a fair system if innocent people are being put to death. It felt good to know that through Townsend's article, more people would hear about wrongful executions. Hopefully, the article could convince them that something must be changed. Capital punishment is not the answer.

Farther on, we received a three-dollar donation from a kind man. He smiled and said we were going to heaven for what we were doing. "If it were that easy to get into heaven," I said, "the roads would be full of walkers!"

Am I going to heaven? I don't know. I'm trying to walk like Jesus, but I'm sure there's more to it than this. One thing I do know is that if I get there, I won't be alone. I guess that's why we have to learn to live in this life the same way we'll be living in heaven: in a community of love. It's all the little details that count—all the little gestures and the attitude with which we make those gestures. They all add up.

Frank parked the van in a breakdown area, and we slept there for the night. Every time a large truck passed us, it shook the van and woke me up, but not Frank. Thank God my kidneys were good. I only had to use the bathroom once before we pulled over for the night. Poor Frank had to go out into the woods a few times in the middle of the night. The next morning, though, we had to move early. My kidneys weren't *that* good!

May 1: Reidsville, North Carolina

I had to keep up my pace. The clouds above looked gray and ready to burst. If I could just make it to the Virginia state line, I'd be happy. And I was close!

Oooh, there goes another Virginia plate! I had been so excited when I saw my first Virginia car tag. Now they were popping up pretty frequently. Soon I would reach Virginia, and these tags will be the norm.

When Jack Payden-Travers called to check on our whereabouts, I joyfully told him that we were about eight miles from Danville, Virginia. That was where Jack was going to meet up with us. I just hoped we could get there before the nasty storm started.

I upped my pace, dreaming about the insoles that would be waiting for me at Jack's place. I'd never needed insoles as much as I need the ones waiting on me. Ha! It may sound carzy, but those insoles would be like gold to me (and my feet).

Moving this fast reminded me of my salad days. Literally . . . of working table to table at the old restaurant. I wonder how many miles I walked per day as a waitress? After work, I was always dead tired. Of course, I didn't have my SAS shoes at the time. Or good insoles.

Ahhhh . . . those insoles are gonna be heavenly!

The rain showed mercy and held off until I got my miles in for the day. I reached my daily goal, and then some. Twenty-two miles, a record! Frank and I "rewarded" ourselves with potato chips, Vienna sausages, orange juice, and another night parked at a gas station. *Good Lord.*

As I digested the tiny sausages, I reminded myself how lucky I was. The rain was coming down hard, but Frank and I had figured out how to park the van in a certain way so it wouldn't leak. That's teamwork. The rain bounced off the roof, and we were warm, dry, and cozy.

"The Lord giveth his beloved sleep" (Psalm 127:2).

May 2: Heading for the State Line

It drizzled all day. I could hear people honking their horns through the sound of the soft rain hitting the hood on my jacket. A few drivers stopped to talk about the issues for which we were trying to raise awareness. A lady in a truck with two little dogs even asked me if I needed a ride.

Everyone thanked me for being brave enough to walk, and thanked Frank for being brave enough to shadow drive. I told Frank after they'd left that they should have thanked me for riding with him. That was the real bravery! Of course, good ol' Frank laughed like a nut. Me? I wanted to cry.

The Bible says the streets in heaven are made of gold. Down here, the highway is made of pennies, nickels, and, if I'm really lucky, sometimes quarters. I spent most of my day looking down at my feet and picking up the lost change. I was extra tired after all that bending down, then standing up, then bending down again. Now, if someone could tell me which highway was covered in paper money, that'd be fantastic?

The trail of lost change led me to a rest area. The maintenance person thought we were there to beg for donations and said we couldn't stay. I explained that we just needed a place to rest for the night, so he left us alone. I should have told him I didn't need to beg. The highway was lined with gold.

"Do not neglect to show hospitality to strangers, but by this some have entertained angels without knowing it" (Hebrews 13:2).

CHAPTER SIX

Virginia

MAY 3, 2005–MAY 14, 2005

May 3: Danville, Virginia

YES! Today was a big day. When we entered Danville, Virginia, I was so excited that I called everyone I knew. We still had miles to go, but this was remarkable.

When I called Mom, she was thrilled. "Oh, Eleze!" she said. "That is wonderful, baby. You are going to finish this walk!"

She passed the phone to my brother Bob. "Hi, Lisa. Bet you just drove up to Virginia!" he scoffed.

Ouch! My own brother just accused me of faking my walk.

"Do you know how hard it would have been to try and fool everyone?" I said. "That would have been more difficult than walking."

He didn't have a response to that. The truth of the matter was that Frank and I had traveled across five states now—732 miles, with me on foot and Frank . . . well, being Frank! How dare anyone accuse us of faking our walk! It hurt my feelings.

After the call, the weather turned sour. I guess it was in sync with my emotions.

Frank and I decided to enjoy the rest of our day and celebrate our arrival in Virginia. We feasted on golden fried chicken and biscuits. Food tasted so good after I'd walked all day. No wonder I still hadn't lost a pound! We got a room at a cheap motel and relaxed for the night with a nice hot bath and TV. It felt so good to be in Virginia!

The most exciting part of our journey started the next day: the final leg to Washington, DC. Our plan was to walk the 245 miles through Virginia in thirteen days. We would stay on Highway 29, which would take us through Danville, Lynchburg, Charlottesville, Madison, Culpeper, Manassas, Fairfax, and Arlington.

"The Lord is my helper, I will not be afraid. What shall man do to me?" (Psalm 118:6).

May 4: Meeting Jack

We met up with Jack Payden-Travis early in the morning. It felt like we were old friends. He was wearing a cowboy hat and blue jeans, and his blonde hair was pulled back into a long ponytail. He looked like a cool hippie. Snazzy. I love hippies!

It was the perfect welcome to Virginia. Jack walked with us most of the day and set us up with some people to stay with for the night. Frank and I both enjoyed Jack's company. He was a good, easygoing person. He filled up our gas tank and treated us to lunch. He also set up an interview with a local newspaper reporter in Lynchburg.

I found my first paper money while walking with Jack. I knew he'd brought me luck! It was a one-dollar bill, but still, I put it away in the tin can where I'd been saving all the change I'd collected so that I wouldn't spend it. Jack said goodbye to us after lunch. I hated seeing him go because, as I said before, it got lonely walking alone. Of course, I knew I had God with me. But He wasn't always that talkative.

Frank and I spent the night at a truck stop. I had walked eighteen miles that day.

Thank You, Lord, for letting us enjoy our day in the company of another.

May 5: Beautiful Virginia!

I felt a bit like Indiana Jones today. I was walking through what I called the "thigh-high highway grass." Okay, maybe the name wasn't all that catchy. But this grass was so tall I felt like I was in a jungle and needed a machete to carve my way through it.

To make matters worse, there were *snakes*. The whole time, all I could think about was a snake slithering up to bite my foot without me even seeing it. I didn't have a machete, but I did have a walking stick/dog intimidator wand. Now it would function as a snake prodder, too! And snake prodding I did. I poked the grass in front of me as I walked down the curvy Highway 29 to Lynchburg.

Yet while this area may have had snakes, the dog situation was contained. Virginia had a wonderful dog ordinance. Unlike South Carolina, all the dogs had to be confined or on a leash. I didn't see any running loose. And the countryside was just beautiful! Everything was so green. The grass especially. The hills rolled into the horizon, where they merged with dark green meadows.

Between the windy highway and beautiful scenery, I got distracted. It was my turn to get lost for a change. Frank almost started yelling at me! I walked about a half a mile before I realized I was heading the wrong way, but I eventually got back on track. When I looked over at Frank, he was laughing like a crazy person. I burst out laughing, too. Why not? We were both crazy with joy that the walk was almost finished.

"And God saw all that he had made, and behold, it was very good" (Genesis 1:31).

May 6: Fine Hospitality

We were rewarded after a long twenty-one-mile walk. Our pit stop for the evening? Jack's house in Lynchburg. He introduced us to his wife, who also happened to be a minister. Several friends, all members of their church, joined us for dinner.

Oh, and what a dinner it was. A feast, I tell you—and vegetarian at that! Salad, corn on the cob, pasta, homemade bread, berry pie, and water straight from the faucet. Poor Frank was like a fish out of water with no meat to eat.

Seeing all of us gathered around the food on the table, sharing and caring, reminded me of the Last Supper. As Norman Wirzba wrote, *"Food is God's love made edible."* That's what it's all about—not just the nourishment, but also the spirit of sharing. It's the *feeling* you get every time you pass the peas or deliver a meal to a needy person, when you tell him or her through your actions, "You are someone for whom Christ died. In His eyes, you are a priceless treasure, worth dying for. I see this. I see you."

We stayed up chatting until Frank and I couldn't keep our eyes open, and then we took our baths and went to bed.

"Let your way of life be free from the love of money, being content with what you have" (Hebrews 13:5).

May 7: Walking for a Cause

After a good night's sleep, Frank and I woke up to a beautiful morning and got an early start. My insoles from SAS shoes were waiting for me on the porch. I installed those babies, and man, what a difference! They could have me walking forty miles a day instead of twenty. Ha!

Of all the states I'd walked through, Virginia had proven to be the friendliest by far. Everyone was fabulous.

"Miss, are you stranded?"

"Can I give you a lift?"

"Is everything okay?"

I'd never had so many people pull over on the highway to ask if I was okay. I wasn't sure why. These folks were, of course, some of the kindest I'd met. But I think it was also because Frank was so far ahead of me—again!

I also had the company of another reporter. Jeesh! I was getting used to these newspaper articles. Local reporter Shannon Brennan wrote a story headlined "Walking for a Cause." I hoped it inspired people and brought hope.

After nineteen miles, we called it a day. Off to good ol' Jack's place again. He invited us to spend another night at his house, and we happily obliged! He took us to his church, where we shared dinner with his Sunday school class. Of course, the food was delicious—fried chicken, green salad, rice, and wonderful homemade desserts. Frank was happy he had some meat to gnaw on.

Once again, the people were *sooo* friendly. They treated us like family. Yeah, that's what it's all about. That's how it's supposed to be. We *are* one family—the human family—and that's how we are called to live. It's not about biology or whose genes we're carrying or whose blood runs in our veins. It's about sharing all we have as brothers and sisters. That is the cause I was walking for.

It was a pleasant change to talk about something other than the issues. Everyone was talking about everyday stuff—their families, their lives . . . you know, just getting to know one another. What a relief to just talk about normal life.

Lord, thank You for the love and comfort of family and friends.

May 8: Challenging the Death Penalty

Shannon Brennan's article made us popular, in Lynchburg at least. Who knows, maybe beyond? After her article was printed, I felt a palpable change in the air. I could sense the difference I was making and see its effects.

When I read the article, I was shocked the paper actually printed what I said: "The death penalty is man's way of playing God." People started to look for us, blow their horns, and stop us on the road just to say hello and wish us good luck. *Hundreds* of people were seeing our signs and showing us their support. It felt incredible!

For breakfast, we stopped at a fast food restaurant and met a nice group of people who had read about us in the newspaper. Frank and I spent some time with them, chatting about the walk and all we were experiencing. Some of them even wanted to take photos with us! No autograph requests yet (ha, ha), but I was starting to feel appreciated all the same.

Then, of course, reality brought me back down to earth. I had just put my pinkie toe on Highway 29, near Amherst, when a local policeman stopped me. "You *cannot* walk on this highway," he barked. "You *will not* walk on this highway."

What was wrong with this man? Didn't he read the newspaper? He wouldn't budge, though, so we had to drive out beyond the city limits (about three miles) and resume the walk.

Of course, my ego bounced back once we reached a road sign that read, "Washington: 164 miles." My eyes filled with tears. It felt so good, and crazy at the same time. I was so close.

I passed inmates picking up debris on the highway. They overlooked a five-dollar bill, which I picked up and added to my money tin. As we went by, they read the signs on the van and gave me a "thumbs up." I could tell they were pleased.

Jack called and said he was out of town, but he'd left us the key to get into his house so that we could spend another night. I can't tell you how good it felt that Jack, a total stranger, had opened his home to us! It was as if he were saying, "I recognize you as a sister, and I welcome you." Oh, it filled me with a bucketful of warm fuzzies.

Opening my home is something I also like to do for others, especially for travelers who can't afford hotels. It seems like so few people are willing to do the same. I guess it's because there are so many con artists out there, and you can never be too trusting. It helps if you're able to check someone's credentials.

May 9: End in Sight

We got an early start today. A bit *too* early for the van, I guess. Five miles into the walk, it started to make a strange, squeaky noise. Squeaaaaaaaak! Squeeee-akkkk! Frank jumped out as if he were trapped inside with a wasps' nest.

The two of us stood staring at the van for a few minutes until a man stopped to help us. "The van might take you to where you want to go," he said at length.

"You think so?" I said.

"Yes . . . or it might not. It's really fifty/fifty."

"Fifty/fifty?" I said.

"Maybe more like forty-nine/fifty-one."

Frank didn't like those odds. He wanted to turn around! But a little car noise wasn't going to make me turn back. No way, no how, especially with the finish line in sight. Besides, I knew Jesus had my back.

I thought we should take a break from the van and have a snack. Okay, to be honest, I thought maybe I could bribe Frank with some ice cream. Ha! While we waited in line, a woman approached us and said she had read about us in the newspaper. She donated five dollars. Her kindness made the cold treat taste even sweeter.

Frank was still not persuaded, however. So we went to a service station to get the van checked, but they told us they didn't work on vans. I told Frank it was time to hand it over to the world's mechanic: God. Our lives were in His hands, van and all. He would take care of things.

We spent the night at a gas station. If Frank's snores were evidence of his anxiety fading, then he'd be good to hit the road tomorrow.

Lord, I am looking at my glass as being half full, not half empty.

May 10: A Nasty Twist

Everything was falling apart. First the van, and now me. I wasn't sure how I managed to do it. I'd walked more than 800 miles. I'd braved dogs, snakes, thunderstorms, and insane drivers. But now *this* was going to slow me down?

As I stepped off a sidewalk, my foot connected with the ground the wrong way, and I rolled on my ankle. Fortunately, at this point a sponsor, Betty Gallagher, and her friend Virginia had joined me on the walk. When I hurt my ankle, Betty went to the drug store and bought a wrap. I was worried. I knew the injury would hold me up.

Betty and Virginia treated us to a lunch of fried chicken and fries. Pretty tasty meal. While we were eating, a woman donated ten dollars. She was full of praise and gratitude for us. I shouted to a man tending horses in his yard, and he came over. He said he had read about us in the paper and stayed to talk for a while.

"Do you really think the President will see you?" he asked.

"I hope so," was all I could say.

"All I know is that if someone walked as far as you have just to see me, I would definitely talk to them. I wish you luck with everything. Please be safe."

Now I would have to replace the word *walked* with *limped*. If the President wouldn't see someone who had walked as far as I had just to meet him, certainly he would see someone who had *limped* all the way. Only time would tell. For now, time was telling me my ankle hurt—and bad!

I limped down the highway and asked God and the Pope to help with the pain. I was stuck with a squeaky van and a creaky ankle. But my heart warmed up once I finished walking and we were on the way to the Gallaghers' house for supper. We heard a car horn blowing behind us, pulled over, and got out. A guy came up and asked if we were from Brewton. We said yes, and he said he was, too. His name was Edward Tate. Yes! A fellow Brewtonian! I can't tell you how happy I was that he'd stopped to say hello. As I said, it's often the little gestures that matter the most.

That evening, we had dinner with the Gallaghers on their back porch while two doe stood in the backyard watching us. The family invited us to stay for a couple nights.

Lord, thank You for the support of familiar strangers.

May 11: Charlottesville, Virginia

Most days we hit the road early. Today was no different. We made it to Charlottesville, Virginia, around noon. I loved the hustle-bustle of college towns. So much energy. I could feel the dreams brewing in the air.

Speaking of air—and airwaves—ABC and CBS interviewed me! I also did a telephone interview with a local paper. George Loper took a snapshot and posted it on his web page. I was featured alongside political articles and commentary.

The reporters wanted to know how the trip was going. "Has there been any moment during this walk that you've wanted to give up?" they asked.

"Absolutely not!" I said. "I'm going to make it to that finish line, even if I have to crawl!" Of course, that wasn't quite true. There were certainly times I wanted to give up. Usually those moments were stressful, heated-type moments that never lasted too long. *Dear Lord.* Maybe I'd be punished by really having to crawl. My ankle was still hurting quite a bit, and Frank was still managing to take the wrong turns.

I was thankful to Chiquita Nettles for the airtime on my cell phone. I don't know what I would have done without it. I was thankful as well to the Gallaghers for their wonderful hospitality. It would be our last night in their home.

Thank You, Lord, for the love and support of friends and strangers.

May 12: Getting Close Now

We left the Gallaghers' home early in the morning. They left us eighty dollars on the dining room table, a tape of one of our interviews, and a note saying goodbye. They had to pick up their son from the airport in Washington. It was his bed that I'd been sleeping in.

My hands were trembling. We were days away from the goal. It was time to call the Capitol to arrange a time to deliver my letter to the President. Of course, I had initiated the walk to change the minds of the people and communities I was traversing, but the President was my final audience. This was the curtain call.

I was directed to Congressman Bonner's office. My mind was racing. I imagined how my meeting with the President would play out. He'd read the letter and listen to what I had to say, his brow creasing with concern about the conditions I was describing. Then he'd promise to do this and that.

"That's not how this is going to happen," said Congressman Bonner's aide.

"I've walked 900 miles to protest hunger and the death penalty. I did this to hand deliver a letter to the President—*my* President—and I . . ."

"You'll have the ear of Congressman Bonner, but not the President, Ms. Thomas." I'd meet with the Congressman on Tuesday, May 17. I would not meet with the President. I considered staging a hunger strike outside the White House, but I let the congressman's aide talk me out of it. I later regretted not doing it. I should have followed my heart.

Still, the long haul was nearly over. I was so close, but the farthest stretch was just coming up. I knew it was a mind thing, but the closer I got to my goal, the longer it seemed to take to get there! So the long plod continued.

Thank You, God, for the strength of my legs and feet to keep me going.

May 13: Tick, Tock . . .

"I was at a meeting in Birmingham when someone mentioned that Alabama was about to execute a man on death row," I recounted to a local reporter on the phone. He had asked why I had decided to walk against the death penalty. "There was almost no reaction from the crowd, and I thought, *Wow! Was no one concerned that Alabama was going to kill this man? How nonchalant are we about the death penalty?* That's when I decided to try to draw people's attention to this serious issue. A human life should never be treated so indifferently."

As I wrapped up the interview, I was reminded why I was walking and who I was doing it for. Whether I met with the President or not did not change the meaningful impact my journey had made thus far and it's unforeseeable impact in the future.

Finally, my ankle injury was healing up—and just in time. I was walking through that tall grass again, and this time it was swarming with ticks! The little monsters were sucking me dry! Didn't anyone mow the grass around there? Oh, the road to the President was full of troubles.

I walked over some beautiful bridges. One was covered and crossed a river; another went over a little brook with wild flowers growing all along the edge. A woman's car had broken down there, and she was standing at the side of the road. I asked if she needed any help, but she had already called for assistance. Later, she caught up with us and brought us cold drinks.

I was really feeling it now. I was close to the end. Jack had arranged for us to stay with the family of a supporter named Mary Grace for our night in Wolftown. She saw us coming down the road, came up to us, introduced herself, and led us to her house. We would have never found it otherwise. Set deep in the woods, it was an interesting place that looked like a log cabin. It had a pond behind it, and it was there that I got to have my first ride in a canoe. It felt like I was sitting on a cloud rocking back and forth. I loved it, even though I couldn't swim.

"Our father, who art in heaven . . ." (Matthew 6:9).

May 14: Gainesville, Virginia

Mary Grace made copies of our letter to President Bush and typed up a statement for the local newspaper in Madison. We left Wolftown at around 6:00 AM. Mary Grace gave us twenty dollars and offered us breakfast, but we decided to skip the meal and just get back on the road. We got lost trying to get back to the highway, so we had to go back to the house and ask her to show us the way.

Jack was trying to set us up at another home, but I told him we didn't mind sleeping in the van. "Well, if you need to get a room, just tell me and I'll pay for it," he offered. I thanked him for his kindness, but I didn't want him to pay for a room when we could stay in the van for free.

I walked to Warrenton, where I was forced to ride the extra ten miles of interstate to Gainesville. We arrived around noon. I was glad to be resting my ankle. I had really pushed myself the last two days, and it was starting to sting.

Frank and I spent the night in Gainesville, Virginia, in the guesthouse of the Benedictine Convent. It had four bedrooms, with a small kitchen and laundry room. We had meals in the convent with the sisters and joined them when they did their evening prayers. The chapel was smaller than I expected, but it had a cozy and intimate vibe that made me feel the strong presence of God.

When it was time to retire for the night, Frank and I had the guesthouse to ourselves. We played around for a bit, yelling to each other from different rooms. I soaked my ankle in hot water to reduce the swelling and watched TV. Frank complained about the food. I told him to suck it up because nobody was going to be cooking pigs' feet for him. I, on the other hand, was loving every bite! Just to be able to eat someone else's cooking—and not even have to wash the dishes!

The closer we got to the finish line, the more exciting it felt. Frank and I discussed what we would do when this was all over. I just wanted to rest, while he wanted to use the money he was earning to buy new clothes. Go figure! I told him he might need to invest in a good pair of eyeglasses, too.

We were going to walk into Washington, DC, the following day. Jack called with early congratulations.

CHAPTER SEVEN

Washington, DC

MAY 15, 2005–MAY 18, 2005

May 15: We Made It!

Today was the big day. Frank and I awoke before sunrise so we could get going as soon as daylight came. This would be the longest and happiest twenty-one miles I would ever walk. I was blessed with sidewalks—never had I been so happy to see cement! It was the first time I felt like I was walking in a city rather than on the open road.

As the traffic zoomed by, I kept imagining how it would feel when my walk was over. I knew for sure that I wouldn't be going on any hikes soon. No Appalachian Trail for me. Ha! I walked straight through the day, only stopping to use the bathroom. My eyes narrowed on the bridge that separates Virginia from DC. My nerves rattled as I approached. It felt like an electrical bolt zapping straight through me.

I crossed the bridge and jumped up and down. "It's over! We made it! WE MADE IT!" Frank grinned from ear to ear. I guess I did, too, because later my cheeks were sore. There was no parade or marching band, though. The walk ended the way it had begun: lonely. If I'd been a movie star or TV personality or a serial killer murdering elderly people up Highway 29, there would've been hundreds of people waiting, including reporters and paparazzi from all over the world.

But it was just me. A poor Alabamian who made less than $10,000 a year, trying to help other poor Americans. We don't get fanfare. We just do what we must do. I won't lie. It was a lonely, sad, glad-it's-over moment.

What an anti-climactic finish.

Sherman Neal, a friend of mine from Los Angeles, put us in touch with John and Betty Branch—friends in Clinton, Maryland—to show us around. We spent the night at a hotel in Virginia. Sister Magdala reached out to Sister Kitty of Baltimore, Maryland, to meet with us and help us prepare for our upcoming appointment with Congressman Bonner. She met with us in downtown Washington, DC, helped us find Congressman Bonner's office, and showed us where to catch the train. We still hoped that if we delivered the letter to Bonner, he would pass it on to the President.

May 17: Meeting with the Congressman

We left the hotel at 6:30 AM to catch the metro into Washington, DC. It was a workday, and the train was crowded. We arrived two hours early. I was so nervous waiting in the lobby. I couldn't read, do crossword puzzles, or anything else except bite my nails.

At last, Congressman Bonner, his aide, and two reporters met with us. We discussed the food stamp program and poverty in Alabama. Even though the congressman had done his homework, the result was the opposite of what I had been hoping for. He felt that too many people who didn't need food stamps were getting them, so the system needed revising. I agreed but begged him to take into consideration the seniors who needed help with food and couldn't get it.

"Congressman," I said, "I've walked 900 miles to deliver this letter to the President. Since I am not permitted to see him, please pass this letter to him on my behalf." Bonner declined. He said he would write his own letter and incorporate some of my thoughts concerning the plight of the elderly and the working poor. He would also note the possibility that innocent people were sitting on death row.

Yikes. I felt like a deflated balloon. I was helpless. It seemed as if I had done all that walking only to end in defeat.

We caught the metro back to our hotel and checked out. And yes, I remembered to tip the hotel maid. We pulled out in our van and started for home, but first we would spend another night with the sisters in Gainesville, Virginia. It was rush hour by this time, and the traffic was dreadful. I decided to drive and let Frank take a break.

May 18: Home Sweet Home

After a good night's sleep back at the convent in Gainesville, Frank and I got up early, had break¬fast, and said goodbye to the Sisters. We drove nonstop and made it to Brewton in fourteen hours! It was hard to believe that a trip that took fifty-three days to walk took only fourteen hours to drive.

The van didn't give us any trouble on the way back, but it died a week later. I know it was God who made sure we got back without anything happening.

So, had I accomplished anything? Perhaps the real question was, did God accomplish anything? I still believe it was Him who sent me on that mission to deliver a letter to a President who did not give me the time of day—or who was perhaps unaware of my very existence. He knows that the solution will not come from those who walk the corridors of power. They have their own agendas. The solution will come from the little people . . . people with the hearts and the wills to truly love their neighbors.

So, the answer is yes, I believe a lot was accomplished. The walk generated a lot of publicity. We got plenty of press coverage and spoke to a number of people. The message was out. In addition, many of the people we spoke to were genuinely interested in trying to do something about the problems in their communities. Countless others read the newspaper articles. Who knows what God will do with that— or what He has already done.

After a couple of days' rest, I settled back into my routine as quickly as I could. Everybody was happy to see me, and I was happy to see everybody. All in all, everyone fared pretty well during my fifty-three day absence. I had spent a lot of time thinking while I was out there on the road. In the end, I realized that my life didn't belong to me. It belonged to God, and God would use it where He needed it the most.

If someone had told me twenty years ago that I would walk more than 900 miles for hunger and a moratorium on the death penalty, I would have laughed and told that person there was no way. But the truth is that nobody knows where God will lead him or her in life.

Sure, there had been some tough moments—aggressive dogs, the vehicle that tried to run me off the road, the van breaking down—but the response had been largely positive. Of all the people that God could have chosen for this trip, I felt so blessed and special that He had chosen me.

PART III

My Feet Do More Talking

CHAPTER ONE

Walking for Darrell Grayson

JULY 2007

I will never forget the sickening summer of 2007. In June, the state of Alabama scheduled four executions during the span of four months. Of the four, there was uncertainty over the guilt of two of the condemned men.

The first execution, planned for July 26, was that of an African-American man who had been convicted of the rape and murder of an elderly woman. Even though he had admitted to the crime, he had been drinking too heavily on the night in question to remember whether he had actually done it. It seems that he committed the acts on impulse, after he and a friend broke into the eighty-six-year-old woman's house with the intention of robbing her.

Darrell was nineteen at the time of his sentencing in 1982—long before DNA testing was developed. He had been convicted by an all-white jury and defended by a state-appointed attorney whose specialty was divorce cases. The attorney himself later admitted that he had been both unprepared for the case and underfunded by the state. Darrell never stood a chance.

The Innocence Project of New York took up the case and tried to get the state of Alabama to do a DNA test on the victim's clothing, but the state refused. I couldn't understand why. What harm would it have done to conduct a test that would have shed light on the crime? After all, a man's life was at stake.

What if Darrell was innocent? What if he was guilty of the robbery but not the rape and murder? If that were the case, it meant the guilty party was likely still out on the streets, able to commit the crime again. This was a definite possibility, because the Innocence Project had a reputation for only representing people they believed to be innocent. They must have had good reason for questioning the conviction.

Even if Darrell were guilty, was it right to put someone to death for one hour of madness—as tragic as the outcome was—when under the influence? Should one drunken act committed in a moment of insanity determine a person's whole life and his or her right to hang onto it? Had anyone bothered to find out what he was like the rest of the time? Isn't executing a person playing God? Given time, this man, if guilty, might have come to the point of repentance. Perhaps he already had. He was a human being for whom Christ died. God wills that all men should be saved, so shouldn't God be given a chance to complete His work with this man?

I knew I had to do something, so I decided to do what I do best: walk. This time, my purpose would be to support those who were already protesting the execution. I would rally further support, make my way to the State Capitol, and stage a protest against the execution. I wanted it to be an informative walk—one that would make Alabamians aware that our state had the highest per capita death row population in the country.

When deciding what route to take, I thought of the Civil Rights Movement, the greatest social movement our nation has ever experienced. The Rev. Dr. Martin Luther King Jr. and his followers staged a walk that started in Selma, Alabama, and ended fifty-one miles across the state in Montgomery. I decided to walk that same route to demand the abolition of the death penalty in Alabama. It would end on the Capitol steps, in time for me to participate in a planned protest that had been set up by various anti-death-sentence groups on Wednesday, July 25. The speakers were going to be Senator Hank Sanders and Kimble Forrester of Alabama Arise.

I wanted people to see the effort we were willing to put into a cause that most people refused to even discuss. I wanted to make it clear that innocent people could be dying at the hands of the state. Surely, no one would stand by and watch an innocent person being put to death? I kept telling myself that if I could just get that one point across to people, their minds would change. But, like my previous walks, it was a lonely exercise.

My journey began on Saturday, July 21, at 9:30 AM. I met with a fellow activist on the steps of the National Museum for Voting Rights in Selma. There was supposed to be a "mass rally" at Voting Rights Park at 10 AM, but when we crossed the Edmund Pettus Bridge, we saw that only a few people had turned up. Sister Judith Smits (1941–2012) of Mobile's Quest for Social Justice spoke about the injustices of the death penalty in our society.

It soon became clear that the reason no one seemed to care if an injustice was being perpetrated in the name of justice was that nobody wanted to be proved wrong. In addition, because the human being involved wasn't anyone they were directly tied to, it wasn't their concern. If it had been a family member or close friend whose only chance to prove their innocence was through a DNA test, it would have been a whole different story. But because it didn't touch them personally, they could sit safely and smugly in their cozy houses, feeling satisfied that the bad guys were being done away with. Didn't they know the saying, "Even the devil loves his own?"

I'd requested a meeting with Governor Riley to discuss the option of performing a DNA test. While I was en route to Montgomery, his office called to set up an appointment. "Hi, Lisa," the assistant said. "This is Governor Riley's office. I am calling about your request to meet with the governor. Unfortunately, Governor Riley is away for business in Mobile and won't be able to make your meeting. I'd be happy to set up a time for you to meet up with his chief of staff, though."

This was disheartening, and it made me worry that the outcome of this walk would parallel the outcomes of my previous walks. I'd really wanted to see the governor himself. "I'll call back in a few days to set up an appointment," I told her.

I later got a call about a rumor that the Innocence Project's lawyers had become upset with me for doing the walk. "Apparently," the person said, "they feel your walk is creating more publicity about you than the cause. They think that if you go through with it, it'll only detract from their efforts."

"Who are these lawyers?" I said. "Can you give me one of their numbers?" I jotted down the number, called the lawyer's office, and asked to speak to the person who was handling the DNA case.

"Hello, my name is Lisa Thomas," I said. "I'm walking for the abolishment of the death penalty in Alabama." The lawyer was silent. I didn't know if it was because he was confused or angry, but I continued. "I just received a call that your office isn't too happy about my walk to press the court to get the DNA test for Darrell Grayson."

"I'm sorry," the man said. I didn't know why he was apologizing. "I haven't even heard anything about anyone walking to get the DNA test."

"Oh, really? Well, I'm trying to meet with Governor Riley to discuss the case and get the DNA test done."

He sounded excited when he responded. "I've actually been trying to meet with Governor Riley for weeks, to discuss the same thing! They always just ignore my calls."

Hah! Didn't I tell you that God works in mysterious ways?

"Would it be okay if I tried to set up a conference call between you and the governor's office?" I asked.

"Yes!" he said. So I called the governor's office and set up an appointment for a colleague and me to meet with Chief of Staff Dave Stewart and Deputy Legal Adviser Scott Rouse on July 25. I also requested for them to arrange a conference call with the Innocence Project of New York.

The morning of the meeting finally came, one day before the scheduled execution. I remained silent throughout and let the lawyers do their thing. One of the points the state argued was that they didn't have the money to do the test (which was false). The lawyer for the Innocence Project immediately shot down that argument by offering to pay all the expenses. He made a lengthy, well-organized plea for the test, but the governor's office would not budge.

I realized there was one obstacle that would simply never budge: a resistant will full of pride and hatred. That is what I saw that day: people who thought they had the power of God in their hands and loved every minute of it. It wasn't just about this man. It was about knowing that they had the power to dispose of a person's life. I call it a "God complex." That willingness to flick a switch and end a life was indicative of a cruelty so horrid it ripped my heart out.

Helplessly watching it all play out in front of me gave me a sick, sinking feeling of frustration and despair. People who are not power hungry will always give others the benefit of the doubt. But if one is at the mercy of someone with no mercy, then there is no hope for justice. As Dr. King said, it's a form of hatred that makes those subjected to it impatient due to "forever fighting a degenerating sense of *nobodiness*."[1] My God, even Pontius Pilate washed his hands clean of Jesus' crucifixion. In the governor's office, I didn't see any signs of concern that an innocent man might be put to death.

Why would any state allow an execution to be carried out if there was even the slight possibility that the convicted person might be innocent? Even those who advocate for the death penalty should want to be certain that the person being executed is 100 percent guilty. What will it take to overcome this callous indifference to human suffering? How many walks will it take to

1   Dr. Martin Luther King, Jr., "Letter from Birmingham Jail," open letter written April 16, 1963.

wake people up? What price must we pay in the meantime? Will it be our brothers, mothers, sisters, fathers, or children the next time? Until we find a better way, we're all at risk. No one is safe.

After the interview—and no doubt after a flurry of phone calls—the governor's office told the media that no new information had come to light that would warrant a stay of execution. As a citizen of Alabama, I was one of many who paid the price for the execution on July 26, 2007—the execution of a man who might have been innocent. We don't know whether he was or not, but not because some of us didn't try to find out.

CHAPTER TWO

Walking for Luther Williams

AUGUST 2007

On August 19, 2007, I set out on yet another mission to delay an execution in Alabama. This time the case was especially unjust, because Luther Williams, the person in question, was possibly mentally retarded.

Williams had been convicted in 1989 of shooting a World War II veteran. Twenty-eight years old at the time, he had been on the run from a prison work-release program. Luther testified that he and two friends had found the victim broken down on the side of the road. Although the murder weapon had later been found among his possessions, he claimed to have been sleeping in the back seat of the car while his friends shot and robbed the victim. The two other suspects pleaded guilty to the crimes and received life sentences.

Like most other inmates, a state-appointed attorney had defended Williams. Regardless of the validity of the case, the state psychologist had testified that the suspect had not been tested for possible mental retardation due to a lack of funds. That argument was so absurd that I was left speechless. It wasn't a *lack of funds* that prevented the testing—it was a *lack of will!* Excuse me for stating the obvious.

Faya Toure joined me this time to demand that the test be done and that the State of Alabama live up to the Supreme Court's ruling that forbids the execution of the mentally retarded. The walk proved to be far more taxing than I'd expected. On the second day, all my backup support disappeared and I couldn't reach anyone on the phone. I didn't know what to do, so I asked God to show me the path forward. He told me to walk six miles, get someone to bring me back to my car, drive back to the point at which I had stopped walking, and then do the same again until the walk was finished.

I didn't know if I had the courage to do what God was asking and walk that far without any sort of shadow driver or partner. If someone had told me that I would be walking by myself, I probably wouldn't have set out. So I sat in my car, hoping for someone to call or come, but they didn't. Eventually, I got up and started walking. I did just as God told me to do: I walked six miles, hitched a ride back to my car, pulled it up to where I'd stopped, and continued the walk. Everyone who took me back to my car signed my walk journal as validation.

That night, I stayed with my sister Molly in Montgomery. I made it to the Capitol and stood with a few other people to protest the execution. Williams was executed later that day. He maintained his innocence until his last breath. After that, I left the death penalty protests up to the experts and concentrated on feeding the living. I realized this cause was bigger than me, and it was both mentally and physically exhausting.

On May 15, 2014, writer Douglas French posted an article about a botched execution in Oklahoma. He noted a study done by *The Boston Globe's* Austin Sarat, who examined the documentation relating to every execution from 1890 to 2010. Sarat found that three percent of all executions were botched, and that lethal injections "are botched at a higher rate than any of the other methods employed since the late nineteenth century—seven percent." The result was excruciating suffering.

"Another new study," wrote French, "using thirty-one years of data, has determined that *four percent of those sentenced to death were innocent. . . . This percentage likely undercounts the number who were falsely accused.*" French went on to quote attorney Clarence Darrow, who wrote in *Resist Not Evil,* "To punish a human being simply because he has committed a wrongful act, without any thought of good to follow, is vengeance pure and simple, and more detestable and harmful than any casual isolated crime."[1]

1   Douglas French, "Barbaric State Vengeance," May 25, 2014, http://www.oanow.com/opinion/columns/article_f149f8a0-dbf6-11e3-b8c8-0017a43b2370.html.

CHAPTER THREE

Feeding College Students

2011

A college freshman looks dejectedly at her class syllabus. She's a political science major, and after she completes her degree, she hopes to attend law school. She's volunteered for a local legal aid department this summer and wants to work on behalf of victims of human trafficking. To get there, she has to take "Introduction to Political Science," a prerequisite for every poli-sci class she needs to finish her degree. Like the introductory class for other majors, this class is part of the general education curriculum and all poli-sci majors are required to take it. To that end, the classes are often taught in an auditorium with hundreds of students in attendance.

That brings us to our college freshman's dilemma. The professor, in an effort to make sure all the students' voices are heard, is requiring the enrollees to purchase a clicker. This is a keypad device that allows students to mark their own attendance, ask and answer questions, and anonymously participate in class discussion. As well, in an effort to comply with the university's new green policies, the professor is using an eTextbook rather than a traditional paper text.

Our college freshman has no objection to the professor's modernized class updates *per se*. She would like the opportunity to participate in class, and she is environmentally conscious herself. But the cheapest clicker she can find is fifty dollars, and because the eTextbook is built into the class fees, it will cost her an extra $120. Being a savvy student, she knows that she could have found a used paper text online for half that amount. She quickly surveys the other classes, hoping to find another section that isn't using the clicker and eBook. However, the university—in an effort to keep the classes uniform and ensure an equal educational for all—has mandated that all po-li-sci courses be taught in the same manner.

Our student has already paid this year's tuition—a staggering amount that twenty years ago would have covered her parents' entire university education. The college savings account her parents set up for her is now nearly depleted. She used her Stafford loan and the money she received from cleaning motel rooms back home to cover her dorm room. She bought her textbooks with a little help from her grandmother. Now she's looking for a part-time job, but with the yearly influx of students to this small college town, jobs are scarce.

Before the fall semester has even begun, she's worrying about how to pay for her spring classes. She doesn't dare dig any further into her college fund, as she needs to set that aside for tuition. Her fall loan is already tapped out and she can't afford the campus meal plan. She had intended to spend the little funds she had left from her summer job on groceries, carefully allotting a monthly amount for food, but there's no other option. Sighing, she pays the extra fees out of her September grocery money. She stockpiles some applesauce and granola bars in her dorm room. That small amount of food will have to see her through the next two weeks.

The Plight of Today's College Student

During the past ten years, college tuition rates have increased eighty percent. While the parents of today's students paid an average tuition bill of $2,500 per year, they are paying upward of $8,000 for a single semester at a state institution. Yet while tuition has increased astronomically during the past twenty years, federal financial aid hasn't. The amount an independent student can borrow, in the form of a Stafford loan, to cover their first year of college is $5,500. This is much the same as it was in 1995.

In the wake of the 2008 financial meltdown, grants and scholarships have become even more competitive for underclassmen, as have college jobs. This financial shortfall has to be made up somewhere. Some students opt for predatory private student loans. Most parents find themselves doubling down on their mortgage or increasing the amount of their Parent PLUS loans (unsubsidized government loans). Other students work multiple jobs, sometimes clocking as many as sixty hours a week to cover their expenses. Still, these efforts to come up with the annual $25,000 for tuition, fees, books, and room and board aren't enough, and students have to make sacrifices. A place to stay and food to eat soon begin to feel like luxuries.

Feeding America is the nation's largest charity devoted to providing hunger relief. They serve nearly 46.5 million Americans annually. Ten percent of those are college students, with two million of those students attending classes full time. According to their 2014 *Hunger in America* study, "Over thirty percent of households spoke of having to choose between food and education expenses on a yearly basis."[1]

One in six American households reports being food insecure, but that number quadruples when it comes to college students. Last spring, *The Washington Post* reported that nearly two-thirds of students at Western Oregon University lacked access to a sufficient quantity of affordable food. In a 2012 survey of undergraduates at the University of California, Berkeley, almost half the students admitted to skipping meals for financial reasons.

In response, colleges have started opening their own campus food assistance centers. In 2008, there were only four in existence, but today there are 121. Still, the assistance these centers offer falls far short of the need, and even students attending colleges with on-campus food pantries aren't always aware they exist. The food assistance programs aren't well advertised, and while students will approach their financial aid counselors about finding money for tuition, they are reluctant to mention that they're going hungry. It seems the stigma attached to social welfare doesn't end at the campus boundaries.

In a society that attaches such great importance to a college education, more needs to be done to ensure that college students are adequately fed. There are numerous studies showing the adverse effects of hunger on children's learning, and the effects of hunger on young adults are no less severe. College students' health, academic performance, concentration, and mood are all negatively impacted by hunger. Students who are food insecure have lower GPAs and higher dropout rates.

The biggest problem with the college hunger crisis is a general lack of awareness of the issue. Students are generally unwilling to confide in their college counselors, and they're even less willing to admit being hungry to peers and even parents, let alone school officials or the media.

---

1   "Hunger in America 2014: Executive Summary," © 2014 Feeding America, http://help.feedin-gamerica.org/HungerInAmerica/hunger-in-america-2014-summary.pdf.

Opening a New Restaurant

My first experience with this problem came just a few years ago. Although finishing college wasn't on my path, I can attest to the many benefits of attending college. Hope College provided me with a safe place to explore adulthood. I lived on my own, made friends, attended classes, and, unlike half the college students today, never went hungry. So I was shocked to learn of the hunger pandemic on college campuses today.

After closing Drexel and Honeybee's back in 2002, I always hoped to be able to reopen a restaurant once the food bank was up and running. Thanks to the efforts of the Brewton community and all our wonderful donors and volunteers, the food bank and meal delivery program were soon thriving. So, a few years back, I was able to realize my lost dream and open a second eatery.

Having enjoyed the hubbub of student life when I was at Hope College, I located the restaurant in the student center of the local community college. Like everyone, I had heard the jokes about college students and their budgets—their penchant for Ramen noodles, their hording condiments from fast-food restaurants, and their likelihood to turn up at a boring after-class lecture if free pizza is offered. In a traditional sense, these are often considered rites of passage, like all-night study sessions and homecoming football games. Students' voracious appetites are often considered a byproduct of their age. After all, when else but in your teens and early twenties can you eat however much you like? We've all heard of the "freshman fifteen," right?

I always assumed that while these students may be eating tubs of peanut butter and snacking at every opportunity, their campus meal plans and their parents kept them adequately fed. I guess I was reluctant to believe the more disturbing rumblings I'd heard: that students weren't filling up on their meal plans, that the rising cost of tuition and books had forced some to bypass the meal plans completely, that they weren't being fed at home, and that while their parents were giving them what they could, there wasn't enough to go around. The ramen, peanut butter, and free pizza weren't "extras" or a quaint joke. It was all those students had.

When I first opened my restaurant, I continued my typical policy of charging three dollars for a hot meal. I was quickly alarmed to see my customers scrambling through their pockets and backpacks for what change they could find. Even three dollars was too much for most of them to pay! As I watched the dining students, I would see a pair share a small bag of chips or cookies. By the end of the semester, many of those youngsters (especially the athletic ones) had lost a noticeable amount of weight. The "freshman fifteen" no longer referred to how much a student had gained; rather, it was a better measure of how much weight the students had lost.

Sadder still, many of these students were probably going to bed hungry at night and then waking up the next day to more of the same. Talking to the students, I learned that many of them didn't have food waiting for them back in their dorm rooms, nor was there a hot meal for them at home on the weekend. Many of their parents were underemployed, if not unemployed, and just keeping their kids enrolled in college was a struggle. I heard story after story of parents losing jobs, families losing homes, or money being tight for any number of reasons. It didn't matter why. The result was always the same: hard times and empty stomachs.

Growing Up with Hunger

I knew how they felt. Growing up with eleven brothers and sisters meant that our parents couldn't afford to pay for the primary schools' hot lunches. So we took our lunch to school with us, usually sandwiches. Having the ravenous appetites of growing youngsters, most of the time I was still hungry after eating my lunch. Luckily, children are generous creatures by nature, and I found comfort among my young classmates.

In second grade, a girl swapped me half her bologna sandwich, decadently kitted out (or so it seemed to me) with lettuce and mayo, for half my peanut butter sandwich. I can still see her little hands tearing into that bread, trying her best to divide the portions equally. I wish I could remember her name, but like so many of the classmates from my childhood, her name is lost in the shadows of time. But I'll never forget the joy of that moment when I realized that angels walk among us.

The middle school cafeteria had an archaic rule that didn't allow us to share our lunches. But that didn't stop my friends Arlene Jones and Brenda Riley from sneaking me the leftovers of their hot lunch underneath the table. It might not sound like much, but even today I can recall how good those mashed-potato and English-pea sandwiches tasted!

We all know that children go hungry. It's a tragic yet unavoidable fact of life—one I hope we can rectify together. But college students going hungry was beyond my experience. After all, as a society we tell our young people to go to college, go to college, and go to college. Doesn't it make sense, then, that as a society we would support them once they're there?

Fortunately, that was my own experience. In the summer of 1969, nine of my classmates and I had the incredible opportunity to take summer classes for four weeks at Northwestern College in Orange City, Iowa. The school didn't have the funding to feed us lunch and dinner, so different families welcomed us into their homes and shared meals with us. It was a wonderful, powerful experience that allowed us to interact with different people from all walks of life and witness kindness firsthand. Every household was different, but they all shared a common purpose. Not only did they feed us, but they also went out of their way to make us feel like we were a part of their family. The families from that summer were one of the many great influences I credit for teaching me what true selflessness is. I often reflect on the kindness I experienced in the face of hunger.

After attending college, I stayed on in Michigan. I was between jobs, and there were days when I had no food to eat. At night I would hang my head out the window of my room and dine only on the aroma of the neighborhood's grills. Tears of hunger would course down my face, and my unsatisfied stomach would rumble as I wondered where my next meal would come from. Hunger can be one of the loneliest feelings on earth, and like so many others of the unseen hungry, I suffered in silence. I know that many of today's college students are doing the same, helpless in the grip of hunger.

Something needs to be done to help these children—for really, in many ways, children are what they still are. They are older children, just on the brink of becoming adults and beginning their life journeys, but they are children just the same. If as a society we believe what we preach—that college is important—then let's give these young students every opportunity to complete their education. We can't let them go hungry.

Feeding Hungry Students

Now when students stop by the restaurant, they eat for free. I set up a donation box on the counter, and patrons are invited to pay what they can. The proceeds go back into the restaurant, continuing the mission of feeding the students whose financial dedication to their college education leaves them short of food.

Three local foundations have chipped in annual donations that help keep the restaurant going. They are committed to the belief that no college student should ever have to go hungry. The restaurant's wonderful volunteers Ola Ball, Doris Crewell, and indeed, all of Carlisa's volunteers, can always be counted on to make deliveries and help out anytime it's needed. And restaurant employee Gloria Dortch arrives at work every day ready to help me battle hunger. I'm always grateful and humbled to learn that awareness of a problem is all it takes to get people involved in solving it.

There are days when the enormity of feeding the hungry is overwhelming—days where, out of sheer frustration, I just want to say, "Forget it!" But usually those are the days when a parent visits a child on campus and tells me how grateful she is for what we are doing. Those are usually the days when a student proudly admits to me that he's the first in his family to go to college.

The work is rewarding, but it is hard at times. There's always a need for more funds, more food, more time, and more volunteers. There always seems to be an unending supply of those who do without. We have managed to establish one small service on one small campus, and other groups are doing similar work at other colleges, but the assistance is falling short of the need. I believe that we are all basically good people and that we all want to do what is right. But I think sometimes other concerns sidetrack us. We're afraid to dive in, afraid to try, afraid of failure. So we wait for an invitation when we should be the ones leading the charge.

As Susan Sontag wrote, *"Do stuff. Be clenched, curious. Not waiting for inspiration's shove or society's kiss on your forehead. Pay attention. It's all about paying attention. Attention is vitality. It connects you with others. It makes you eager. Stay eager."*[2]

I pray these stories inspire you to help. I pray you take this as an invitation. Maybe, like my summer class families, you'll open your home to a group of college students and share your Sunday dinner with them. Maybe you'll have pizza sent to a dorm just for the thrill of committing a random act of kindness. Or maybe you'll take a bag of groceries to the university's food pantry, knowing that your donation may be all that stands between a college student and an empty stomach. You'll likely come up with some other wonderful solutions. When you do, I hope that you'll share them with me and with others. Together, we can put an end to this beast called hunger.

2   Susan Sontag, commencement address delivered at Vassar College in 2003, quoted in Sam Dillon, "Commencement Speeches; Reflections on War, Peace, and How to Live Vitally and Act Globally," *The New York Times*, June 1, 2003.

PART IV

Random Acts of Kindness

CHAPTER ONE

Reflections on Kindness

I don't feel no ways tired.
I come too far from where I started from.
Nobody told me the road would be easy.
He brought me too far to leave me.

Rev. James Cleveland, "I Don't Feel No Ways Tired"

I'm sure even the most prepared of marathoners approach the starting line with a bit of doubt. And though I wouldn't be running, my fifty-three-day walk from Brewton, Alabama, to Washington, DC, was no less daunting a task. To combat those inevitable moments of doubt when fatigue, monotony, and the sheer distance of my walk threatened to overwhelm me, I made a list of moments that inspired me. This was a list of random acts of kindness that unearthed the miraculous in the everyday and kept me moving toward my goal.

Beginnings

On the first day of my walk, just the idea of undertaking such a long journey seemed nearly impossible. But then I remembered Johnny Rowell, a newly released prisoner who was working to rebuild his life. His journey was one that must have seemed similarly impossible to him.

When I first met Johnny, he had neither food nor money and seemed lost in a life he'd been thrown into with few resources to help him manage. With the gift of just a few groceries and twenty dollars from Carlisa, Inc., a grateful Johnny was better equipped to begin his long journey back to reentering society. By the time we parted, he was already looking for opportunities to contribute back to the community by offering any help to the charity that he could.

I realized that if Johnny could successfully undertake such a long and difficult journey, I could as well. So, with Johnny's inspirational story in mind, I began my walk.

Impossible Journeys

Of course, even journeys that seem impossible are possible with a little help. So many journeys that I have witnessed could have ended abruptly but were continued with a little assistance from others. Consider the following examples.

A man came by the food bank one day looking visibly upset. When we asked what was wrong, he shakily replied that his mother, who lived in Evergreen, had fallen. The man was desperate to visit his injured mother, but he didn't have the gas money to make the thirty-three-mile trip. We were able to find gas money for the man, and this small family was reunited.

A college student approached customers at a local gas station. She was desperate to make it back to her college classes, forty miles away, but she was out of gas and out of money. Through an impromptu and generous donation of $100, she was able to return to school.

A lady in our community named Mattie was diagnosed with breast cancer. She had very little income and no car to take her to and from her treatments. Given her financial state, she certainly couldn't afford someone to carry her back and forth to her appointments. But miraculously, money arrived at Mattie's every week, and she was able to get to her treatments.

Once when I was visiting my mother at the hospital, I had the occasion to meet another daughter who also visiting her mother. Unlike us, this pair wasn't local, and this poor, frazzled daughter was searching for a way to get herself and her mother back to Monroeville, Alabama, which was about forty-five miles away. She had just been laid off, and between the job loss and caring for her mother, she didn't have gas money for the return trip. Another small bequest for gas and the treat of a lunch cheered up this overwhelmed woman and helped her and her mother make their way home.

I wonder if these individuals know that their stories helped me on a seemingly impossible journey of my own.

Small Steps

When there are so many miles to walk, one step seems almost insignificant. And yet, in the end, it's all those small steps that get us where we're going. When working to help the hungry, it always seems there's an endless supply of empty stomachs but a finite amount of food. All the donations we receive help us manage this challenge.

One time, during a particularly rough financial patch, I received a twelve-dollar donation. While that may not seem like much, at that time it was invaluable, as it helped the mission carry on for another day. When it started to seem like another step on my walk wouldn't make much of a difference, I reflected on that twelve-dollar donation and how it led to another day.

Endurance

I soon found that the secret to walking such a long way was simply to put one foot in front of the other and repeat the process, over and over and over. It was a surprisingly easy trick to master. Of course, we've all practiced this maneuver in our daily lives. Sometimes, when life is particularly tricky, just continuing is a feat in and of itself.

One holiday season, a friend told me about a family in which both the husband and wife had been laid off. Like so many others during tough economic times, they had no immediate prospects for jobs, and Christmas was quickly approaching. The couple had four daughters, and they were likely scrambling to provide some measure of Christmas cheer for their children.

The family began receiving money anonymously in the mail. On Christmas Eve, Santa also stopped by with gifts for the entire family. This was only fair, of course, given the four girls were always well behaved—just what Santa likes to see! I realized that if this family could carry on, I could as well. All I needed to do was continue to put one foot in front of the other.

Miles Ahead

For most of my journey, I was always seeing the road waiting for me up ahead—the miles I had yet to walk. To cope with that vast expanse, I thought about the random acts of kindness I could do for others. For instance, each time I stopped by the local donut shop, I bought an extra donut for the next customer who came in the store.

Wrong Turn

Getting lost is often part of a long journey. When I think about misplaced steps, I have to smile, a bit bemused, at a trick my friend Ruby and I once tried to play on a waitress at a local pizza eatery. When the waitress brought our bill, Ruby and I, feeling mischievous, looked at the tab and exclaimed, "Oh no!" The waitress asked if anything was wrong, and we replied we didn't have that much money.

Unbeknownst to us, the poor waitress had already had one table duck out on a bill, and the manager had made her cover the check. So the waitress, not picking up on our jest, offered to loan us the money to pay for our pizza. We were touched by her offer of a loan to two complete strangers. Hoping to atone for our ill-timed joke, we quietly paid our bill, the walkout's bill, and left a generous tip.

Missteps can be retraced, and many wrong turns can be set right. Each time I found myself lost on the walk, I remembered that kindhearted waitress.

Partnerships

I wouldn't have been able to walk all that long way by myself. As in all things, partnerships helped see me through.

One of the best partnerships I've forged is with Mr. Junior. One day, I passed by a house that had a huge pear tree growing in the yard. I had been on the lookout for pears to make preserves and cobblers, so I stopped to see if the owner would be willing to part with any of his crop. Mr. Junior was the homeowner, and he generously told me that I could have them all.

Mr. Junior was an elderly man. He was on oxygen and had noticeable tremors. In exchange for the pears, I offered to deliver a hot meal to him daily as I went about my route. The deal delighted him. Thanks to our wonderful partnership, I have a constant supply of pears, and Mr. Junior gets a hot meal each day.

I couldn't help but think of Mr. Junior as I enjoyed the company of my walking partners.

Refreshment

Walking is hungry business, so I was immensely thankful for any refreshment offered along the way. One time, I stopped to talk with a group of prisoners who were laying blacktop on the highway. The guard allowed me to offer snacks and drinks to the seven men hard at work, and the men greatly appreciated the gesture.

Now that I have tasted (on a small scale) the rigors of being out on the road for an extended period of time, I can more fully appreciate the thirst and hunger that comes from a long day's work. It made me more fully value the time I spent with these men, and I'll never again view a road crew the same way.

Energy Boost

Unsurprisingly, there were days when the road seemed more uphill than downhill and one mile felt more like ten. My steps felt deflated, as though I were a car hobbling along on a flat tire. It reminded me of the time I overheard a young woman's conversation during a shopping trip.

The woman needed to visit her doctor in Florida, which was about sixty-five miles away. But she was nervous about making the drive, because the back tire on her car was worn to the point of being unsafe. When she exited the store, Carlisa, Inc. was waiting with the money to fix her tire.

I was blessed to be a part of the transaction, and as I drove away, I spotted in my rearview mirror the woman happily jumping up and down. That image of sheer, impulsive joy gave me the energy to walk on. I even had a bounce in my step.

Following

Following signs . . . following maps . . . following the road. My journey was carefully laid out for me, and to get me where I needed to go, I only had to follow the directions I was given. It's always easier to find the way when you have a good example to follow. In our ministry, we have an abundance of them.

After hearing about our food bank on WEAR-TV's *Angels in Our Midst*, one woman started sending us twenty-five dollars each month. Her donation continued for two years, until she was laid off from her job and was financially unable to continue her monthly gift. Our ministry followed her example and sent her money each month until she found a new job.

The road signs telling me which direction to go made me think of this donor, our angel, in my midst.

Those Who Walk Beside Us

Sometimes we become so involved in our own difficult journeys that we forget others walk beside us. On one such day, I tried to avoid a certain cashier at a grocery store. Her line was the only one open, but I was reluctant to approach her because I thought she was overly chatty.

The woman noticed my reluctance, but despite my slight she was pleasant. She asked how I was doing and thanked me for having my groceries so neatly organized on the counter. It was then that I noticed a hint of sadness in her eyes. Ashamed I had hurt her feelings over a minor—and harmless—personality quirk, I decided to make amends by quietly leaving her twenty dollars.

The woman followed me out of the store, thanking me tearfully. She said the funds would help her a great deal, given her present circumstances. But her kindness was of far greater benefit to me, because it reminded me that we all travel rough roads at times, and we can do so with grace and compassion.

Observance

It is easy to feel unnoticed on the road amidst the cars and travelers zipping by intent on their own destinations. The feeling reminded me of when my best friend, Annette, was in love. As her birthday approached, she fervently hoped her sweetheart would remember and mark the day in some way. However, I suspected that her beloved probably didn't remember it was her birthday.

I couldn't bear to see her disappointment, so my friend Linda and I pooled our resources and headed to the nearest flower shop. Once there, we purchased what roses we could afford and left the bouquet in front of Annette's door. The card simply said, "I didn't forget"—a well-meant subterfuge that left Annette to form her own conclusions.

She was so excited about the surprise roses. Later, she fell ill and passed away at the too-young age of forty-two. But she kept the roses—dried memories of a happy birthday that didn't go unnoticed.

I smile as I think of those roses, and I know that my walk isn't going unobserved. Annette is watching me now.

Encouragement

There were days on my walk when I was feeling disheartened. The distance and my purpose seemed too far out of reach. But during those moments, I would remember a man I once met at a flea market.

This man was selling odds and ends, nothing priced more than five dollars, and it was obvious he needed a break. We gave him fifty dollars, and in exchange asked him to donate fifty dollars' worth of merchandise to Goodwill. The transaction provided him a bit of encouragement that lifted his spirits without hurting his pride.

I thought of this man driving to Goodwill at the end of the day, doing a good deed of his own. Now the man at the flea market is the one encouraging me.

Remedies

Small blisters, sore toes, aching legs—these are realities of walking a great distance. Thankfully, an icepack or a well-placed bandage can go a long way toward curing many ills. But not all ills are so easily remedied.

One day when I was enjoying a glass of tea in Huddle House, one of my favorite restaurants, I overhead a woman talking about a visit she'd made the previous night to the emergency room. The attending doctor wrote her a prescription that she didn't have the money to fill. The medicine didn't cost a large amount, and I was fortunate enough to be able to help her out with the funds.

Norman Vincent Peale said, "When you discover the wonders of giving, you will wonder how you ever lived any other way." That is the secret to life: *give so that you might receive.* Now I found that the woman's prescription was a remedy for my own woes, and remembering her story helped ease some of my own aches.

Good Weather

Anyone who has lived in the South can appreciate humidity, and there were days when the stagnant air and unrelenting sun threatened to derail our walk.

I often daydreamed about cool breezes and refreshing rain.

Once, in a slight fit of impetuousness, I noticed I had sixty one-dollar bills in my purse. I had just finished lunch at my favorite restaurant and was feeling particularly cheerful. I tossed the dollar bills into the air and watched as the ceiling fan scattered them around the room. The shocked patrons instantly came to life, scrambling to grab a bit of this impromptu lottery. Smiles abounded as the money rained down. But none were bigger than mine, as the thrill of the moment was infinitely more valuable to me than the money I had let fly.

The exhilaration I felt as I left the restaurant after having participated in that dollar rainstorm stayed with me on the walk, and the memory of that particular rain shower helped get me through the hottest days.

A Different Point of View

It was hard not to notice my surroundings as I walked on the road. Scenery that normally shot by through a car window became minutely observable on the day-to-day walk: a small patch of flowers growing wild, a bird singing from a fence post. The world was different up close.

It reminded me of a woman whose son passed away after a long illness. We met happenstance in the grocery store as she was on her way to buy a black dress for the funeral. Feeling helpless in the face of a mother's despair and desperate to ease some of her suffering, I asked if she would let me buy her dress for the funeral. I hoped I could recast her heartrending errand as a gift from a friend.

And so, when the walking became tedious, I tried to remind myself to find some small bit of beauty around me, to look at things from a different point of view.

Good Habits

Although the purpose of my journey wasn't fitness, with all that walking my thoughts did occasionally turn to exercise. When my thoughts wandered, as they are prone to do, I recalled news stories surrounding the obesity epidemic in young children and reflected on the importance of establishing good habits when we're young.

Once, I had the pleasure to meet a young boy named Kenneth, who came by the food bank with his mother. We were fortunate enough to be able to give Kenneth twenty dollars. We wanted to arrange a surprise for his mother, so we asked Kenneth to take his mom to Burger King and buy her lunch—a request I'm sure Kenneth happily complied with. Not only did the pair share a treat of a mother-son lunch out, but Kenneth also learned the habit of giving to others.

Good habits, too, are hard to break.

Partings

Eventually roads part, and we find ourselves heading in different directions from those of our friends. Audie, a former classmate, was terminally ill with cancer. When I went to visit him, all he could manage was a warm smile of greeting. Audie's daughter worked two jobs to help pay for her father's care, and Carlisa, Inc. helped where it could. At each crossroads we passed, I thought of Audie and his warm smile.

Healing

As the walk went on, I spent a little extra time each evening soaking my tired feet and massaging my exhausted legs. When minor pains interfered with my daily miles, I would remember a young man who had been seriously injured in a car accident.

I heard about the young man through a benefit his family held. They sold fried fish dinners to raise money to cover his medical expenses. The fundraiser was doubly beneficial, as thirty of those fried fish dinners were purchased and delivered to the elderly and the disabled.

This small act, which helped heal the woes of multiple people, also helped me during the walk. Comparatively, my small aches were trivial to what this young man suffered, and I was able to soldier on.

Favors

Help sometimes comes from the unlikeliest of places, and the walk to Washington was no different. Whether with words of support or a cool drink of water, people seemed eager to help me on my way. But then again, most people look for chances to help others—they only need to be provided the occasion.

Each day when I wake up, I ask God what I can do to help someone else, and He blesses me with those opportunities. Three elderly people visited my restaurant one day and ordered three meals with quiet smiles. It broke my heart when they tried to pool their nickels and dimes together to pay the nine dollars they needed. I told them I needed to give away five free lunches that day and asked if they could help me out and take their meals for nothing. They agreed and thanked me for their lunch.

I hope they know how thankful I was that they allowed me a kind deed—one that left me smiling the rest of the day. I thought about that deed during my walk north.

Walking Partners

Sometimes it's easier to commiserate with those who share our experience. Six months after I lost my mother, I was struggling to cope with her passing and confided in a young employee at my favorite grocery store. She had lost her mother the year before, and she understood what I was going through.

Our talk soon turned to other things. I learned she was trying to find full-time employment, because she was having a hard time making ends meet on her part-time job at the grocery store. I tried to give her a little cash to help her through this rough patch, but she refused to take it. She felt that there were others who could benefit more from the donation.

Finally, after ten minutes of haggling, I convinced her to accept the gift. She assured me that she would pass the blessing on. There is no doubt in my mind that she did. What she didn't realize was that she had already immensely helped someone: me. As I replayed this story in my mind, her inspiration helped me to continue on.

Hope

The walk to Washington, DC, was defined by hope: hope that it would do some good, and hope that our elected officials would hear our message. When I think about hope, I remember a woman I met at a Baptist church fundraiser. The church was holding a yard sale, and the proceeds would be used for the church's youth group.

The woman was elderly and in a wheelchair. She was a member of the congregation and had donated some of her hand-knitted work for the sale. I listened as she eagerly told a potential customer how she made her hand-crafted items and how long it took her. The woman's eyes glowed with hope that someone might cherish an item she'd worked so hard on.

I wanted to purchase one of the knitted white tissue holders, but I didn't have any money. So I made a point to tell her how beautiful the crafts were. The next week, when I was blessed with extra funds, I got into contact with her and made arrangements to buy some of the goods I'd been forced to pass on the week before.

The woman was so excited, and I was grateful I had the opportunity to keep that hopeful spirit buoyed. Just the thought of her smile kept my hopes afloat and my spirit uplifted during that long walk.

Unexpected Destinations

Although we often have our destinations in mind when we begin a journey, sometimes our wanderings can take us to unexpected places.

I once received a referral for our hot meals program. A concerned neighbor had called about an elderly woman she felt would benefit from our services. I promised the caller I would follow up, and so I did. Imagine my surprise when I discovered the woman was an old friend! She was as shocked as I was and confided that I had been on her mind for the past few days. "Doesn't God work in mysterious ways?" she mused.

Indeed He does. Sometimes He knows best where we need to be, and He does what He can to get us there.

Journey's End

As we approached Washington, DC, I knew our long journey was nearing its end. Sadly, I remembered Miss Helen. She was one of my best customers. The last time I had spoken with her, she had told me she was having a surgical procedure and wouldn't be in for a while. This type of conversation was nothing out of the ordinary. Miss Helen assured me the procedure was nothing to worry about and that she would return soon.

I heard nothing for three months. I wondered how the surgery had gone and how Miss Helen was doing. Then one day, a local real estate company called and asked if I could collect some posthumously donated items from a house that was for sale. I stopped by the home, and among the donations,

I found a book with Miss Helen's name in it. I called the realtor, and she confirmed that Miss Helen had passed away unexpectedly.

I was stunned and saddened by the news, but I knew God had provided the book to give me the closure I needed. I thought about dear, sweet Miss Helen during my last steps into Washington.

Support

I exchanged stories with passersby on my way to Washington, DC, who were curious about the walk. These accidental spectators became my impromptu fans, cheering me on the way and offering words of encouragement.

Their support reminded me of how blessed I was to be a member of the Brewton community and the entire world. The food bank receives donations from community members—donations that keep the food bank afloat and allow it to continue its mission. Neighbors approach me when I'm shopping and donate money to help purchase groceries for the food bank. The youth of the First Presbyterian Church banded together to raise fifty dollars on the food bank's behalf.

Once, when the food bank had little more than hotdogs to offer its patrons, I walked out to my mailbox and found an envelope with $250 in cash and a note that simply said, "Thank you." This wasn't the only time the food bank received such timely anonymous support. We also received a $100 bill in an envelope postmarked from Montgomery, Alabama. The enclosed note said simply, "For your mission."

Another time, while on a shopping trip, a man approached me and, in good humor, asked what I was going to do with all the food I had in my cart. When I told him about the problems of students going hungry on college campuses and that the food was going to be used to feed students at the local junior college, he immediately donated fifty dollars to our cause. Another kindhearted soul who overheard our conversation chipped in $150 of his own.

Without the support of total strangers, I know that I would never have finished the walk. And without the incredible support of a generous community—and compassionate and generous people who remember us when they have a little extra to spare—none of the stories on my list would have been possible.

CHAPTER TWO

Reminiscences on Kindness

Writing this book has allowed me to engage with the past. Often, as I sat trying to find the words I wanted, my mind would wander. I would recall the times that made my life of giving worthwhile—moments that taught me happiness can be found in the face of sadness and tragedy.

My life is not unique in that respect. We all have moments of great joy and great sorrow. But isn't it funny that years later those moments of happiness keep providing us with happiness, while those moments of sadness fade just a little bit? We smile as we reminisce about past Christmases, family gatherings, and sharing meals with friends. We still laugh about jokes long since told and the funny things our children said and did as they were growing up. Our brother's impression of Uncle Fred makes us giggle even when he's not around. And we all remember those people who inspired us, if only for a moment: the man who stopped to change a pregnant woman's tire, the teenage girls who shaved their heads to support a friend undergoing chemotherapy, the woman in the store who helped a lost child find his mother.

Even the sad moments are recast in our memories, and with time we are able to find a bit of the positive in them. We all mourn the passing of a grandparent, but our memories become a celebration of their life. We hate to reflect on moments when we failed, but those moments provide us with insight that helps us lead a more productive life. Even in the face of the worst possible catastrophes, we have a bit of pride when we remember how our community banded together to help the family who lost their home in a mudslide, or the firefighters who rushed into the burning building, or the countless people who reached into their pockets to donate what they could to help rebuild a town after a devastating tornado.

Writing this book meant I took a trip through my past, but my trip wasn't a straight line. Instead, I followed a meandering path, letting my memories take me where they would. I remembered happy times and sad times, times I was angry and overwhelmed, and times when I was overcome with joy. I am blessed that those joyful times outweigh the sorrowful ones, and it is these reminiscences that helped inspire this book. I want to share them with you now.

Mr. Miller

Some of my fondest memories are of Mr. Miller, a dear man who often stopped by the food bank. He was a regular for groceries, and he was also on our list of people that we helped with gas money so he could go to his cancer treatments. He always tried to bring a cooler full of freshwater bream to give to others to show his thanks and gratitude. When Mr. Miller's wife died, he donated all of her adult diapers and bed pads to Carlisa, Inc. His donation helped several of our clients.

Mr. Miller was diagnosed with an aggressive type of skin cancer, and his frequent visits allowed me to see the damage the cancer was causing. I watched as the disease ate away portions of his fingers and hands. All too soon, he was battling several other types of cancer. Mr. Miller eventually underwent surgery in an effort to control the disease, but he couldn't afford the special bandages and medications he needed for the skin grafts. Mr. Miller had always been so generous with us, so we were happy to repay his kindness by donating the funds for his medical bandages. Although he fought bravely, he passed away after a long battle. His death left a deep emptiness in my heart, and I miss his visits to the food bank immensely.

We often hear about the high costs of health care, and we watch as our leaders struggle to find a solution. But what if the solution lies with us? Mr. Miller's diagnosis of cancer represents the catastrophic medical crisis we all fear, but he taught me that with a small amount of assistance, no one has to go without some form of help. When I am told about others in similar situations, my memory of Mr. Miller quickly inspires me to go to their aid. Each time that I do, thoughts of Mr. Miller and his cooler of brim always make me smile. No amount of help is ever too small. In fact, the smallest acts of kindness can reap the biggest rewards.

Wife of a Soldier

What about the wife of a soldier fighting in Afghanistan who had a new-born son and no way to pay her light bill? The young woman's parents didn't approve of her interracial marriage and kicked her out of their house, leaving her alone to fend for herself and her infant son. She came to the food bank, eyes full of fear and humility, and quietly confessed that she had no money. She was embarrassed to ask for help, but the thought of her seven-week-old child being left in the dark compelled her to come to us. We were thankful for the opportunity to help the family of a soldier who had sacrificed so much for us and provided the young lady with a check to pay her electric bill.

We often wonder how we can repay our soldiers' sacrifices. Our hearts ache as we watch them leave their young families behind—as we see their children tearful at the airport, not knowing when Daddy or Mommy will return. We want them to know they're in our thoughts and prayers as we see them spending holiday after holiday overseas, missing Christmases and birthdays, family get-togethers, and anniversaries. Each day they face danger on our behalf, all so that we can rest easy. We can do our part by taking care of their families in their absence.

Soldiers and their families are sacrificing the precious time they have together, and sometimes that's little enough. They shouldn't have to sacrifice anything else.

Snook

I met Snook and his mother at a yard sale. Snook's worried mother quietly told me that he had been beaten so badly that it had caused him permanent brain damage. Currently, Snook was homeless. He had multiple health problems, and he was battling a drug addiction.

Snook's mother did her best to care for him, but she knew he needed professional help. She was desperate to get Snook off the streets, and finding her son shelter was the first step in improving his situation. She was saving for a trailer, thinking that if Snook had some small space of his own it would keep him safe. She was hopeful that she would meet her goal soon.

We felt blessed to have the opportunity to provide assistance and help make up the gap between what Snook's mother had and what was needed. She was able to move Snook off the streets, and he had a home of his own for the first time since the assault. Snook later passed away, but I was glad that he had been able to find a little peace before he departed.

Acts of violence unnerve us all. We feel powerless in the face of such random destruction. But we can restore the balance of life by fighting evil with kindness. Kindness helps us reclaim society's humanity. Kindness lets evil know that it can't have the last word.

Oh, Lord, open the hearts of all Your children to help people like Snook.

Firecracker

One morning, I was delivering food boxes to an elderly woman. A puppy sat on her front porch waiting to greet me. He was afflicted with mange so severe that his little red coat was hardly visible.

"Excuse me, Ms. Rosa, is this your dog?" I asked as tactfully as possible. "He looks very sick and needs medication. Do you mind if I try to help him?"

Ms. Rosa, feeling guilty over the pup's neglected condition, confessed she felt terrible that she hadn't the means to help her tiny, four-legged friend and readily agreed to any assistance available. I visited the vet and described the puppy's appearance. The vet kindly prescribed a small bottle of medicine and told us to bathe the puppy with the treatment daily. I returned to Ms. Rosa's, medicine in hand, and together we gave the puppy a bath. Ms. Rosa promised to continue the regimen until the mange had cleared.

A month later, I saw the puppy again. He was cured and a little ball of energy, playfully bouncing around the yard chasing after his ball. As I watched the exuberant pup bounding about, I quietly named him Firecracker. He was the prettiest redheaded dog I'd ever seen.

Abandoned Dogs

Firecracker wasn't the only dog I had occasion to help. One time when I and some others were visiting a garage to collect goods that had been donated to us, we discovered four abandoned dogs. They were starving. They stared at us with large, vacant eyes, their skin hanging off their bones in an exhausted way. They were completely emaciated, and I wondered how they had managed to survive for so long. The ground was littered heavily with scavenged bones, likely the remnants of a deer they had killed. It had enabled their survival, and suffering, just a bit longer.

We quickly bought some dog food and fed and watered the dogs. I immediately called animal control, but because they were overwhelmed and had limited resources, they wouldn't be able to look after the dogs for a few days. So, for that time, I kept feeding the starved dogs until animal control could pick them up.

There are countless other dogs and animals out there that also need our help. God put the animals into our care, and giving extends to them, too. My fear of dogs makes it difficult for me to approach them (though, in Firecracker's case, I do make exceptions), but fear can't deter us from our mission of kindness and generosity. There are few things more uplifting than the purr of a kitten or the happy wag of a dog's tail.

Flip-Flop Customer

The flip-flop customer. The soles of his shoes had separated from the tops, so his arrival was always announced by the "flap, smack, flap, smack" of his steps. My own feet were blessedly clad, and my heart yearned to help him. No one appreciates the benefits of good footwear like a waitress, and though I was a tad bit afraid to approach him, after a week my conscience wouldn't let me listen to the flapping and smacking anymore. I decided to take a chance to offer my help.

"Excuse me, sir," I ventured, "but I'd love to buy you a new pair of shoes. Your poor feet deserve shoes that are whole. What size are you?"

The man was silent for a few moments, almost as if he didn't remember what his shoe size was. "I think . . . I'm a 10½," he murmured softly, almost questioningly.

That same day I went shopping and found him a new pair of brown loafers. When I saw him the next day, I happily presented him with the shoes. "These should help out," I said. "I hope they give your feet some rest."

When the man went to put on his new shoes, I noticed that he didn't have any socks. Shoes need socks like cookies need milk, so I casually mentioned that I would bring him socks the next day.

"Thank you, thank you!" he said, his voice trembling. He put his new shoes on, and he wore them home that very day. His next visit to the restaurant was with happy feet rather than a "flap, smack."

From the time we're young we're taught the lesson of self-sufficiency. But while independence may be a virtue, it teaches us not to ask for help. I don't think that's the lesson God wanted us to learn. If He didn't want us to help each other, why did He make so many of us? Wouldn't He just have plopped us all down on our individual deserted islands? We may be afraid to offer assistance to those who need it, but I'll bet they're even more afraid to ask. Remembering this elderly gentleman gives me the confidence to approach others in trouble and offer what help I can.

John

Small gifts that reap big rewards remind me of my friend John. John only had two dollars, but he donated them toward the burial of a young man who had been killed in a car accident. Like so many people, John didn't have any burial insurance, so he empathized with the young man's family. "Whenever I die, I'm probably going to need help with my burial, too," John reasoned.

We appreciated John's gesture but laughed at his reasoning. We assured him that he could count on us when his time came. We didn't realize that John's time would come all too quickly. Six months later, he suddenly passed away. As I remember his two-dollar donation and the last words he said to me, I can't help but smile when I think of all the friends that came together to lay him to rest. I think what brings me more solace than anything is that John knew they would.

Kind gestures needn't be grand. I know it's easy to feel like the few dollars we hand a young mother who is short on her grocery tab doesn't mean much. Or that the handful of coins we give to the Salvation Army each Christmas will be quickly forgotten. But those groceries keep a family from hunger, and so many others add to that handful of change we give that the Salvation Army is able to clothe and feed people the world over. When we stick together and give what we have, it doesn't matter how much or how little is the amount. What matters is that we gave. What we do can change the world.

Oh, Lord, give it back to these young folks in spades!

Ms. Molly

Beautiful flowers remind me of Ms. Molly, an eighty-six-year-old lady I visited a few years back. "I just want to look out my bedroom window," she would continually lament. "I just want to see something pretty."

"When I was young," Ms. Molly would recall, "my family wasn't able to have a pretty yard. The closest thing to a flower garden I've ever seen are the printed flowers on flour sacks and calendars." My heart ached for Ms. Molly, for I knew she spent countless hours at home alone.

A few days later, seizing an opportunity the Lord provided me, I snuck over to Ms. Molly's place when I knew she would be at a doctor's appointment. I carried with me a variety of flowers: gerbera daisies in shades of white, pale yellow, and light pink; loud orange, yellow, and red zinnias; and firehouse red roses. I planted the colorful array right outside the window. When Ms. Molly came home and saw her new flower garden, she was so happy that she cried. During future visits, she was excited to tell me about the beautiful butterflies that visited her flower bed, the fast-moving hummingbirds that stopped by every day, and even the bees that dropped by to get their fill.

Loneliness seems to be an affliction of the elderly as much as arthritis or memory loss. As we age, we say goodbye to our parents, our siblings, our friends. Sometimes it may feel as though we're the only ones left, and loneliness can be far more painful than our aching joints or tender backs. Ms. Molly loved her daily visitors and was comforted by the presence of butterflies, hummingbirds, and bees. If ever you think you can't make a difference, visit someone who's lonely and you'll prove yourself wrong.

Michelle

I think often about Michelle, a co-worker who came all the way from England in the pursuit of the American dream. She was in an abusive relationship in which her boyfriend beat her. I watched as Michelle came to work with bruises and black eyes. I knew that she didn't need judgment—that was freely offered to her (and countless other victims of domestic violence) on a daily basis. Instead, I invited Michelle to my home. Michelle stayed with me for four months until she was able to get her own place. My house felt lonely after she left, but I was happy that she was rebuilding her life.

We all know someone like Michelle, and we're often tempted to turn away. The good in us doesn't want to believe that what was supposed to be love can go so wrong. Maybe that's why we're tempted to blame. We want a reason, but sometimes there just isn't one. But while we might not be able to explain the problem, we can be part of the solution. Finding fault continues the cycle of violence; it keeps the victim isolated and enables their abuser.

Compassion, on the other hand, can be the lifeline someone needs to find his or her way through the darkness.

Kindness, not judgment, is a far better remedy in healing ills.

Mrs. Cooper

I chuckle when I think that maybe I should have asked Mrs. Cooper to be one of my shadow drivers! Mrs. Cooper was one of my favorite seniors. She'd drive herself to the food bank to get groceries even though she was in her nineties. She never had a problem parking in the driveway, but once she did, it was near impossible for her to pull out!

Once the groceries were loaded into her car, Mrs. Cooper would hand me her car keys and ask me to turn the car around for her. When we got the car facing toward home, she would climb back behind the wheel and drive away. Watching Mrs. Cooper putter down the road, I would say a special prayer not only for her but also for the other folks traveling on the highway!

I know that God has a sense of humor, and I'm sure He laughs kindly at us as He watches us bumble our way through life as best we can. I'm also sure that while He enjoys a good chuckle, He gets the most happiness from watching us help each other.

Peanut Brittle Man

It's often the small treats in life that provide us with a bit of unexpected joy. This reminds me of my Peanut Brittle Man. I met him while delivering groceries to his home at the behest of the Department of Human Resources. He was terminally ill and lived in a small trailer with his wife. When I arrived, he was rocking back and forth in his recliner. As he watched the groceries being unloaded, he kept talking about his craving for peanut brittle. He mentioned the buttery treat at least half a dozen times.

By the seventh or eighth mention, I asked, "Can your teeth handle peanut brittle? Are you allowed to have it?"

Excitedly, he nodded yes. "I have such a strong taste for it," he entreated.

I was amused, and the chance to brighten someone's day led me to procure some peanut brittle for him. Oh, if only you could have seen the delight on that old codger's face as he chewed on his treat! It made my heart swell.

All too often I've heard people say that the poor who receive handouts should be grateful for what they get, even if what they get is not what they need or want. But when you give the poor any old thing "they should just be grateful for," you don't experience the kind of joy my Peanut Brittle Man gave me. Giving should be done in the right spirit, in an effort to bring joy and not in an attempt to deride.

The Waitress

Once when I was dining out with a friend, we noticed that our waitress had served three tables but none of her customers had bothered to tip her. She was a good waitress, as far as we could tell. Her service was prompt, and she was friendly. It was disheartening to watch her face fall each time she cleared a table and found no tip. We decided to leave her three dollars for each table, including our own. Her service was well worth it, and it was such a delight to watch her face light up!

It can be disheartening to see others doing the wrong thing. A sidewalk teems with people, all walking by a man holding a sign that reads, "Hungry. Please Help." What do we do? Which example do we follow? Do we ignore the man? Endure that nagging bit of guilt rather than act alone?

Don't be afraid to stand apart. Every kind act can undo an unkind one. We can create the selfless world we imagine.

Woman at a Garage Sale

It does my heart good to know that even those who are in need often think of others who are worse off than they are. It reminds me of a middle-aged woman I would see on my way to work. She was holding a garage sale, and for two weeks straight she spent every day in her yard, hoping to sell some of the wares she had on display. Every day as I returned home, I glanced at her tables, but nothing ever seemed to be missing.

Unable to bear the sight of her unsold goods any longer, I stopped by and announced that I would take the lot. My only caveat was that the woman would take my purchases to the Goodwill store and donate them. She agreed, so I pressed $200 into her hand.

She immediately protested. "No please," she said, "it isn't worth that much! I only need $100." She put $100 back in my hand, kindly squeezing it for a few seconds to say thanks. Whether she was thinking of me or others whom the $100 could help, I couldn't say. What I can say is that she wasn't thinking of herself. That said it all!

Tow Truck Driver

One rainy day, a carpenter came over to do some work for the food bank. When he went to leave, he found that his car was hopelessly stuck in the mud. There was nothing we could do but hire a tow truck to pull him out. I didn't want to burden the carpenter with a tow fee after he had been so kind to help us out, so I asked a tow truck driver who lived in my neighborhood what he would charge to do the job. To my shock, the man replied, "You are so good to my grandmother. I can't charge you anything." As it turned out, he was Mrs. Cooper's grandson!

Imagine if that were how the world worked! Unfortunately, it doesn't work that way yet, so for now those who give and receive freely know a different sort of wealth: they're rich with the pure joy that comes from kindness and sharing. They're rich in a sense of community connection and knowing mutual empathy. Quite simply, they know the pure joy that comes from loving one another in practical ways.

It's not even always about money or food. Sometimes it's as simple as giving people a smile when they look down-and-out or listening to what they have to say. I learned this during my walk to Washington when I met different people on the highway. All some of them wanted was a listening ear. When you reach out to others, they are encouraged to reach out to the world in turn.

Gardens

When I think about my dad, I always remember the huge gardens I helped him plant when I was growing up. One day I asked, "Dad, why do we need such a big garden?" He answered that we would not be the only people to eat from it. He was right. Everyone in the community, at some point, ate something from that garden.

Milk-and-Eggs Lady

"Don't be a hypocrite," I often silently admonish. There are far better examples in life to follow, such as the Milk-and-Eggs lady. An acquaintance of my co-worker Mr. Moore, the Milk-and-Eggs lady lived in Evergreen, Alabama. She had milk and eggs delivered to her by a local meals program. The program was generous to excess, giving her far more milk and eggs than she needed or could even use.

So my co-worker tried to convince the lady to donate the extra food to Carlisa, Inc., where it could be used to help feed the poor rather than go to waste. But the woman refused point-blank. "I don't believe the food will actually be used to help anyone," she heartily stated. Then one day, my co-worker came in all smiles, hauling an armful of milk and eggs. She'd finally been able to convince the woman with the help of a newspaper article about the food bank. What a pleasant surprise! We used the milk and eggs to make desserts and cornbread for our senior meals.

It's really an ironically simple principle. If you say no initially but relent and help anyway, you make people happy. You ease a little suffering. On the other hand, if you promise to do something and don't follow through, people feel hurt. Rather than ease suffering, you add to it. Broken promises are unkind and exhausting. Sometimes, I'm sure you'll agree, it's not the physical things that wear us down but the mental ones.

A Community Effort

Feeding the poor is a community effort—a little taste of what heaven must be like. It's a struggle to keep groceries in the food bank, to keep the elderly and hungry fed every day. In the past, there have been times when our money has run out, when the need has exceeded the financial resources. Sometimes people call asking for food, and we have to tell them that we just don't have any. On occasion, our hot meals are skimpy. One time, all we had to deliver were hot dogs.

So, all the little donations and all the community help we receive are a Godsend. Once when I was shopping for groceries with little money in my purse, I confided to my friend Avis Milton that I was short of cash. Avis immediately reached into her pocket, pulled out a treasure of money, and handed it to me. I was very thankful.

The community is willing to help us out with even more than just money. For instance, if our meat is about to expire, the butcher from one of our local grocery stores will call and sell us some at a discounted price. (Some of the kindness shown to my dad about the expired food has now been passed on to me.) I freeze the food sold to us and serve it at a later date. The kind-hearted people at the local Ford dealership have also donated smoked turkeys and hams that fed many people.

On one memorable occasion, Betty James and her mother heard about our food needs and donated a half-freezer full of chicken. Dr. Smith, for whom my father did yard work during his younger years, sent a donation to help out. I was so thrilled and proud to tell him I was Earlie Thomas's daughter, but deep down inside I think he already knew whose daughter I was.

I'm also thankful to our fire chief, who donates hams for us to serve on Christmas Day. To the local medical center and Longevity Antiques that allow us to set up donation boxes inside their businesses so people can donate to Carlisa. To the club that always donates their surplus food from the Blueberry Festival and other community events. To the local realty company that donates left-behind items from homes that we then pass on to people in need.

On one occasion I received a wonderful donation from a local insurance agent that was right on time. We were down to almost nothing when the man donated $800 to help feed the local college students. His donation was a Godsend and went a long way. A lawyer in our community also always donates to our holiday meals program.

The staff at our local newspaper, *The Brewton Standard*, do everything they can to get the word out about community feeding events and fundraising efforts. They do whatever they can to help, which has made them an invaluable asset to our community. In fact, the entire community has gotten involved . . . they are all ready and willing to do something to help someone else.

Often it's the little things in life that make the biggest difference. A few days before I left Brewton on my walk to Washington, DC, my Aunt Mattie Gantt gave me a simple lightweight jacket with a hood. I had no idea when I decided to take it with me how much of a lifesaver it would become. I wore it almost every day while on the road. On wet days it kept me dry, and on cool days it kept me warm. Like that small gift, the daily gifts of the Brewton community keep me going.

Sophie

Sophie was an elderly woman who was fighting cancer. On the days that she was able to go out, rain or shine, she would come into the restaurant for a hot meal. Sophie liked to order our homemade meatloaf, mashed potatoes, and fried cornbread.

Sophie always insisted on paying, but I would slip in an extra piece of cornbread with each meal. She enjoyed the tea that we served, so one time I promised her that the next time I went shopping, I would buy her a canister. Sophie made it in the following week, and I gave her the tea. Of course, she wanted to pay, but I insisted that it was on the house. You can't pay for a gift!

Sophie passed away just a month later. I know she didn't have enough time to finish that canister of tea, but I was thankful I was able to make that little gesture to show her that I cared. It's fanciful, I suppose, but it makes me smile to think that her family may be sharing a glass of tea this very evening and reminiscing about Sophie.

Why do I think about her now? Because Sophie taught me that if you want to do something for someone, don't wait or it might be too late. You can't let it rain on your parade.

Visitor in Town

A business associate working in Mobile, Alabama, once asked if I knew of a place where a young man visiting Brewton could stay while he was in town. I asked if he knew the young man, and he said he did. He vouched for the boy, saying he came from a respectable family. I told my associate that the young man was welcome to stay in my home. He stayed with me for a week. I was well rewarded for my little act of kindness: he repaired the car and cooked a few meals to show how grateful he was for the help. My biggest reward, though, was making a friend for life.

Woman on a Bus

I think back many years ago to a trip I took on a Greyhound Bus when I was heading back to college. A lady with three small children boarded the bus at a stop in Montgomery, Alabama. After we had travelled some distance and changed buses to continue our trip, the new bus driver asked the woman for the ticket for the smallest child. She told the driver that she didn't have one, but that she would hold the small child in her lap if necessary.

The bus driver told her no and demanded that she pay five dollars more to stay on the bus. Tearfully, the lady told the driver that she had no money.

She begged him to let her hold the boy, saying that the small child wouldn't take up any additional space on the bus, but the driver insisted that he needed the money. I was a college student, so it was a miracle that I even had twelve dollars in my own pocket, but I could see that I would be this mother's only recourse. I parted with five of my dollars so the boy could have a ticket.

Some things in life are just worth more than the price of a ticket.

Dog Taxi

One day I drove past an elderly gentleman who was walking in the blistering heat carrying four bags of groceries. I stopped and offered him a ride. He gladly accepted and asked if I minded if his dog rode along with us. I didn't want to leave a dog alone in the heat, so I swallowed my fear and assented. However, I must have missed the *s* on the word *dog*, because when the man called out, five dogs came running. They all jumped happily, a pile of wagging fur, into the back seat of the car. All I could do was look at them and say, "All right, everybody, let's buckle up."

Unemployed Father

A father who had been laid off was visiting his daughter, who was ill. He gave what little money he had to his grandchildren so they could buy school supplies, which left him short of gas money for his return trip home to Birmingham. While we couldn't give him his job back or heal his daughter, we were able to provide him with gas money.

I suppose kind gestures like this sometimes feel as if they're not quite enough, but healing one small hurt can lead to fixing bigger ones. Hope and kindness are the basis of all remedies.

Woman in the Trailer

I recall an elderly lady who lived in a small trailer. The trailer wasn't winterized very well, and the woman always grumbled about how cold she was. We covered the windows and doors with heavy plastic. It warmed the trailer, and her spirits, tremendously. When I think about her, I realize how blessed I am even when my home feels too cold or too warm. During the times I want to complain, I think about all the people like her who are trying to keep warm in the winter or who are in need of a cooling unit to keep them cool during the hot summer months.

"I Love You"

A man in the twilight of his years who'd had to say goodbye to too many of his friends was dining at my favorite restaurant. He sat at another table, looking sad, mourning his latest lost friend. I wanted to take his mind off his friend's passing, so I told him I loved him. He looked shocked, but he thanked me for telling him. Ever since that time he and I have shared a special friendship.

About a week later, a childhood friend of mine named Claudie Gulley approached me in the same restaurant and said, "I love you, Lisa." Like my elderly friend, I was surprised, but it made me feel good. I thanked Claudie and told her I loved her too. Even though most people will not respond with, "I love you, too," most will respond with a thank you. I have learned to appreciate the thank you and move on.

Hungry College Student

I think about the college student who came back for seconds one day. I asked him if he was still hungry, and he said he was taking something to eat later on. I asked if he had food in his dorm room, and he told me no. When his mother dropped him off at school, she did so without any food or money. She simply didn't have any to spare, because she did not have any money to send him off to school to begin with. We made sure the student had food to take back to the dorm.

Annie

You know you have a friend when you have to come up with $1300 and that friend offers to borrow the money from their credit union for you. My friend Annie stepped up as my guardian angel and did that for me at a time when I had nowhere else to turn. I will always remember her kindness.

True Givers

I fondly remember two sisters who donated five dollars to the food bank. They looked so happy being able to help feed the needy. Both sisters have since passed away, but it still puts a smile on my face when I remember what they did.

And what about Mr. Sanders, one of the elderly clients to whom we delivered hot meals? When I was ill, he sent me a very sweet get-well card. Inside the card, he had tucked a ten-dollar bill. It meant the world to me, because I knew that while he didn't have much money, he had made the decision to be a giver.

When people choose to be givers, it doesn't matter what or how much they give. All that matters is *that they give*. This isn't a dress rehearsal. This is real life, and we all need to do our bit to make the world a better place for everyone.

∾

I've had a lot of bad moments in my life, but I've also been blessed to have many good ones to counter them. When those bad memories skirt across my mind, I quickly think of one of my many fond memories and put the bad ones out of my head. At my highest point and my lowest points, all is well with my soul.

In my life, the most money I made in one year was a little more than $15,000. That figure might cause some people to shake their heads and say, "You poor thing." They might wonder how on earth I lived off that amount of money. It certainly was my parents' wish that I do well—seven of their twelve children earned a college degree.

Yet while I never pursued a college education, I've lived very well. I've lived happy because I lived my life the way I wanted to: free. Along the way, I helped out people in any way I could, and in turn God always looked out for me. I have always heard people ask, "What about your retirement in your old age?" My pat answer is, "God is the best retirement plan anyone could ever have."

Do you have fond memories? Share them with us at

www.pleasebelievepeoplearehungry.com.

CHAPTER THREE

What I Know Now

What I know now is that when those kind white strangers stopped me and blessed me with that Kennedy half-dollar all those years ago, they set my entire life in motion. The wondrous feeling I experienced when they put that coin in my hand changed my life. The feeling was so magnificent that it has been my wish ever since to pass it on to others.

One day when I was driving down that same road where my life had been changed, I saw a boy playing. He looked to be about seven years old. I stopped the car and rolled my window down. "Hello," I said. "What's your name?"

"Hi," the boy replied. "My name's Jacob!" His politeness made me smile.

"I'm Lisa," I said, extending my hand. "Thank you for being so friendly. Don't ever change that." His hand met my own, and I pushed a five-dollar bill into the center of his palm.

"Thank you!" he said, a huge smile plastered on his face. Then he turned and ran off, just as I had done all those years back. I sat for a moment and silently prayed that he would be as blessed as I was with the ability to love unselfishly and bless others.

As I watched that boy run off, I realized that I was doing what I was destined to do. I was being what I—and what everyone else, really—was destined to be. I was able to finally answer my mother's lifelong question, "What do you want to be when you grow up?"

It took a critique of this book by Catherine Y., a total stranger, to put into words what I have been trying to say my entire life: "I don't see much organization. There are many anecdotes that seem to be placed as you think of them. They have a random feel like a butterfly flitting from flower to flower, but barely spending any time on each. We normally flip-flop from subject to subject in our own minds, but readers need to be able to follow your line of thinking and see relevance between the jumps."

This one paragraph sums up the total of my life before I decided to stay on course and follow in the steps of Jesus. All those years since that couple appeared in my life for that brief moment, God had this life in the plan for me. My wealth is derived from loving other people, and that exceeds the wealth of any billionaire.

Bible teacher Joyce Meyer said it best: *"The more you do . . . the more you're able to do. The less you do . . . the less you're able to do. Don't just admire what others do. . . . You do something! You might have to try out different stuff to find what fits . . . but we all need to have a dream and the heart of a finisher."*

Some Practical Pointers

I invite all of you to join me on this rewarding road of alleviating poverty, not only in our country but also in the entire world. My sincere hope is that these stories touch you, because caring for the poor and doing something about their plight leads to immense joy. Find ways to ease someone else's suffering and share in their joy, because joy is and should be infectious. Once you catch it, my hope is that you will become a joy junkie just like me! Once that joy is your goal, nothing can stand in your way.

Whether or not you have money to give, there are a million ways you can help to ease the suffering around you. The following are just a few ideas I have come up with through my own experience with the poor. I am sure you can come up with many more, but this will get the ball rolling.

Practice Fundamental Giving

Every human on this planet has the same elementary need: to be loved and accepted. Whatever else you might do for someone, remember that acknowledging their existence and their value is the most basic thing you can give. Sometimes, all people need is proof someone else cares enough to be interested in them and takes the time to acknowledge them. It could be as simple as a friendly greeting or smile—one that says, "I see you. You are not alone." Your smile has the power to make a sad person's face light up.

If you feel comfortable doing so, take it a little further and chat for a bit. Take a few moments to talk to the person who takes your order at the drive-through. Get to know the office cleaner at your work, or the janitor, or the security guard if your building has one. If they aren't particularly friendly, remember they could just be having a bad day. Don't let that discourage you; being pleasant could cheer them up.

If you pass people and you like their perfume or cologne, tell them. Take time to exchange a few words and find out about their lives. Chat to the poor lady on the bus or train who is sitting alone and looking like she is carrying the weight of the world on her shoulders. Talk to the man next to you in the waiting room who looks like he is expecting terrible news. Talk to the beggar in the street who is so far from hope that his eyes just stare without expectation.

By doing simple things, you are throwing a small pebble of kindness into the big ocean of humanity, and it could create a positive ripple effect.

Look and Listen

Chatting to people will also put you in a good position to discover what their needs are. Most people are too embarrassed to ask for help directly, so you have to develop a "nose" for need. That means simply keeping your eyes and ears open. Notice the road workers pounding away in the heat? Bring them some cold drinks and thank them for the job they're doing. See the frail old lady struggling with her grocery bags? Offer your help to carry them! That miserable-looking person in the elevator might say he is fine if you approach him, but he will still appreciate the fact that you care enough to ask.

If the person does tell you what is wrong, you might be able to do something to ease his or her suffering. If not, maybe you could find someone who can—or at least you could advise the person on where to get the help they need. I'm an excellent eavesdropper, and I suggest you become one as well. Open your ears when you hear people talk about their needs, and if the need is something you can help with, offer to do so. Don't wait to be asked.

Sometimes, people's pride causes them to be reluctant to accept financial assistance from strangers. In such cases just tell them that they can pay it forward when they are in a better position. The main point is that you need to keep *your* eyes and ears open. If you see or hear about a need and have the resources to help, offer it. Of course, this means you will often have to have the courage to approach total strangers. But over time this won't be too difficult for you, because it will become habitual to engage with others. Remember that strangers are just friends you haven't gotten to know yet!

If it is still too hard for you to approach strangers, start with the needs of someone familiar—a relative, friend, or even the office cleaner or janitor when you have gotten to know them. You will be surprised at what you might find out about them. Perhaps you could help alleviate the pain of a cleaning lady. Buy her some pads for her knees or medicine to ease her aching. Perhaps you might notice that her eyeglasses are taped up on the sides and keep falling off while she is trying to work. You could leave her a prepaid certificate for new glasses.

Or maybe you notice the janitor has been working outside in the cold rainy weather all winter long with flimsy sneakers on his feet. Leave him a gift voucher for a pair of boots. Remember you don't have to do it alone. Ask your co-workers to help, and give the certificate for new shoes as a thank-you gift from everyone. I guarantee you that it will lift your heart, and they will feel so appreciated!

Offer Non-Financial Help

Most of the examples I have given so far have a financial component. Although I have funds from Carlisa, Inc. to help out people, I feel much better when I can give from my own pocket. If you don't have any money to spare, look and listen for situations that don't require hard cash. Here are just a few examples:

- Why not offer your time, just as you did when you were a kid, by helping with chores or keeping old folks company?

- What about that lady standing at the bus stop with you in the cold who is wearing nothing more than a light jacket? Offer her a coat that you don't wear any more.

- Perhaps you have seen that old widow who lives down the road struggling along with a walker. You have noticed that her front yard is overgrown. Why not offer to mow her lawn at no charge?

- Do you enjoy gardening? Plant some flowers in someone's garden or teach him or her how to grow vegetables. Get your local nursery involved and ask them to donate supplies. Do an entire street makeover. You have no idea how much the poor crave beauty. If you do something like this for them, you will be feeding their souls.

- Do you have a particular skill such as plumbing, carpentry, or tech? Dedicate a certain number of hours every week to use those skills to help out someone who can't afford to pay you.

- Do you own a restaurant? Give away free meals to the needy when you notice that it's a struggle for them to pay.

- Are you a caterer? Donate any leftovers to a nursing home, a food kitchen, or a group home. Can you imagine the delight a bunch of foster children would experience if they received a feast of finger snacks left over from an office function—delicious bites they'd never tasted before?

- Do you prefer to offer your time in a more structured way? Then volunteer at a charity organization cooking meals, washing dishes, serving food, or doing whatever else is needed. Boy, I could do with some help myself!

Offer Financial Help

If you have a good job and some money to spare, there is plenty you could do with it. Of course, "if you can afford it" is a relative expression. You might have to be prepared to give up buying a luxury item you've had your eye on in order to give to someone with a real need. I generally buy only what I really need and give the rest away. I can assure you the joy that comes from giving will make those small sacrifices worth it.

Because I do this, it seems my needs are always met. I am so hooked on the happiness I experienced when I got that Kennedy half-dollar that I can never resist sharing the little money I have with those who desperately need it. Here are some other ways that you can offer financial help to others in meaningful ways:

- If you see someone having a yard sale, stop and see what's available. If you don't see anything you want, buy a little something anyway. Help the person out. Odds are they are having the yard sale because they desperately need the money. Alternatively, buy all their stock and donate it to a charity store.

- If people come to you selling something they really need, it means they are in despair. Pay for the item, but tell them to keep it anyway. Ask if there is anything else you can do to help. Watch out for people like sweet Carolyn, an elderly lady who set up around town trying to sell different types of merchandise. I stopped and talked to her one day, and she told me how hard life was because of her heart trouble and diabetes. Nevertheless, she had to get out there and hawk her belongings, because she needed the money. She even told me she had to drain gas from her sister's lawnmower to get to her doctor's appointment. I was able to make arrangements to get gas and food donated to her.

- If you've got time, take someone a hot meal—perhaps someone like one of the elderly folks I have described in this book. Do this several times a week, if possible. Work out an affordable grocery list and buy the items when you do your own shopping.

- Buy dog food regularly for hungry animals.

- Indulge in the odd extravagant gesture. Notice the old woman in the restaurant counting her pennies to see what she can afford? Tell your waitress to have the woman order whatever she likes, because a customer has offered to pay for her meal. Do it anonymously and watch her face glow when she gets the message. Observe her looking around the restaurant trying to figure out who it is. I did that once, and it was such fun!

Celebrate Special Days

On Mother's Day, honor a mother—especially someone elderly who doesn't have anyone. Take her a meal or some flowers, or invite her to your home to share your celebrations. The same goes for Father's Day. Or play Father Christmas (or Mother Christmas). On special holidays, sponsor a dinner for those in need. Ask the owner of the local meeting hall to donate their facilities for the event.

Remember the Homeless and the Convicted

Don't judge the homeless, even if they have a drinking or drug problem. You don't know how they got there. While they are among the most vulnerable and sad members of the human family, they are still members of your community. Never give addicts money, because that will just enable them to destroy themselves, but show them you care with a warm blanket, a bit of conversation, or a hot a meal.

Finally, don't forget the folks in jail. Encourage those states that still have the death penalty to give God a chance to finish His work with each of His children. If they are guilty, life in prison means they can't hurt anyone else. Believe it or not, it is cheaper to keep someone in prison for life than to execute him or her. Support the efforts of Project Hope to abolish the death penalty as well as The Innocence Project.

Consider helping ex-cons get back on their feet. I know that people are often nervous about engaging with such people, but they should be allowed a second chance after doing their time. If society shuns them, they are more likely to turn to crime again. You will be surprised how many people do give back, either in kind or money. That's how it should be: everyone helping one another and always having each other's backs.

Start a Joy Revolution!

Let's build a world in which we recognize that every person is a treasure loved by God and is worthy of being loved by us in his or her own right. Let's build a world in which everyone cares for everyone else. If we can achieve a culture of caring, no one will go hungry and we will be rich in ecstasy as we enjoy a little taste of heaven on earth. It is a communal effort, but it begins with you and me.

Remember that being kind to others should never be a random act. It should be a lifestyle.

—Lisa McMillan

Visit our website: www.pleasebelievepeoplearehungry.com